Empire and Constitution in Modern Japan

SOAS Studies in Modern and Contemporary Japan

Series Editor

Christopher Gerteis (SOAS, University of London, UK)

Editorial Board

Stephen Dodd (SOAS, University of London, UK)
Andrew Gerstle (SOAS, University of London, UK)
Janet Hunter (London School of Economics, UK)
Barak Kushner (University of Cambridge, UK)
Helen Macnaughtan (SOAS, University of London, UK)
Aaron W Moore (University of Edinburgh, UK)
Timon Screech (SOAS, University of London, UK)
Naoko Shimazu (NUS-Yale College, Singapore)

Published in association with the Japan Research Centre at the School of Oriental and African Studies, University of London, UK.

SOAS Studies in Modern and Contemporary Japan features scholarly books on modern and contemporary Japan, showcasing new research monographs as well as translations of scholarship not previously available in English. Its goal is to ensure that current, high quality research on Japan, its history, politics and culture, is made available to an English speaking audience.

Published

Women and Democracy in Cold War Japan, Jan Bardsley
Christianity and Imperialism in Modern Japan, Emily Anderson
The China Problem in Postwar Japan, Robert Hoppens
Media, Propaganda and Politics in 20th Century Japan, The Asahi Shimbun Company (translated by Barak Kushner)
Contemporary Sino-Japanese Relations on Screen, Griseldis Kirsch
Debating Otaku in Contemporary Japan, edited by Patrick W. Galbraith, Thiam Huat Kam and Björn-Ole Kamm
Politics and Power in 20th-Century Japan, Mikuriya Takashi and Nakamura Takafusa (translated by Timothy S. George)
Japanese Taiwan, edited by Andrew Morris
Japan's Postwar Military and Civil Society, Tomoyuki Sasaki
The History of Japanese Psychology, Brian J. McVeigh

Postwar Emigration to South America from Japan and the Ryukyu Islands,
Pedro Iacobelli
The Uses of Literature in Modern Japan, Sari Kawana
Post-Fascist Japan, Laura Hein
Mass Media, Consumerism and National Identity in Postwar Japan,
Martyn David Smith
Japan's Occupation of Java in the Second World War, Ethan Mark
Gathering for Tea in Modern Japan, Taka Oshikiri
Engineering Asia, Hiromi Mizuno, Aaron S. Moore and John DiMoia
Automobility and the City in Japan and Britain, c. 1955–1990, Simon Gunn
and Susan Townsend
The Origins of Modern Japanese Bureaucracy, Yuichiro Shimizu
(translated by Amin Ghadimi)
Kenkoku University and the Experience of Pan-Asianism, Yuka Hiruma Kishida
Overcoming Empire in Post-Imperial East Asia, Barak Kushner
and Sherzod Muminov
Imperial Japan and Defeat in the Second World War, Peter Wetzler
Gender, Culture, and Disaster in Post-3.11 Japan, Mire Koikari
Empire and Constitution in Modern Japan, Junji Banno
(translated by Arthur Stockwin)

Empire and Constitution in Modern Japan

Why Could War with China Not be Prevented?

Junji Banno
Translated by Arthur Stockwin

BLOOMSBURY ACADEMIC
LONDON • NEW YORK • OXFORD • NEW DELHI • SYDNEY

BLOOMSBURY ACADEMIC
Bloomsbury Publishing Plc
50 Bedford Square, London, WC1B 3DP, UK
1385 Broadway, New York, NY 10018, USA
29 Earlsfort Terrace, Dublin 2, Ireland

BLOOMSBURY, BLOOMSBURY ACADEMIC and the Diana logo are trademarks
of Bloomsbury Publishing Plc

First published in Great Britain 2021
Paperback edition published in 2022

Copyright © The Estate of Junji Banno and Arthur Stockwin, 2021

The Estate of Junji Banno and Arthur Stockwin have asserted their
right under the Copyright, Designs and Patents Act, 1988, to be identified as
Author and Translator of this work.

Cover image: Ancient Harmony, 1925 (no 236), Klee, Paul (1879-1940) / Swiss,
(oil on cardboard), Gift of Richard Doetsch-Benziger, 1960 / © Bridgeman Images |
Shape © Shutterstock

All rights reserved. No part of this publication may be reproduced or transmitted
in any form or by any means, electronic or mechanical, including photocopying,
recording, or any information storage or retrieval system, without prior
permission in writing from the publishers.

Bloomsbury Publishing Plc does not have any control over, or responsibility for, any
third-party websites referred to or in this book. All internet addresses given in this
book were correct at the time of going to press. The author and publisher regret any
inconvenience caused if addresses have changed or sites have ceased to exist,
but can accept no responsibility for any such changes.

A catalogue record for this book is available from the British Library.

Library of Congress Cataloging-in-Publication Data
Names: Banno, Junji, 1937-2020, author
Title: Empire and constitution in modern Japan: why could war with China not be
prevented? / Junji Banno; translated by Arthur Stockwin.
Description: London, UK; New York, NY: Bloomsbury Academic, 2021. | Series: SOAS
studies in modern and contemporary Japan | Includes bibliographical references and index. |
Identifiers: LCCN 2020055569 (print) | LCCN 2020055570 (ebook) | ISBN 9781350136212
(hardback) | ISBN 9781350136229 (ebook) | ISBN 9781350136236 (epub)
Subjects: LCSH: Constitutional history–Japan. | Japan-Foreign relations. |
Constitutional law–Japan. | Imperialism.
Classification: LCC KNX2101 .B36 2021 (print) | LCC KNX2101 (ebook) |
DDC 342.5202/909041–dc23
LC record available at https://lccn.loc.gov/2020055569
LC ebook record available at https://lccn.loc.gov/2020055570

ISBN: HB: 978-1-3501-3621-2
PB: 978-1-3502-4040-7
ePDF: 978-1-3501-3622-9
eBook: 978-1-3501-3623-6

Typeset by Deanta Global Publishing Services, Chennai, India

To find out more about our authors and books visit www.bloomsbury.com
and sign up for our newsletters.

"Professor Junji Banno, the author of this book, sadly passed away in October 2020, so that he will not see his book published in English. As his translator and long-term friend, I wish to pay tribute to one of the greatest historians of modern Japan".

Contents

Introduction	1

Part I The beginnings of 'Empire' and 'Constitution'

1 Defeating China – towards a 'small empire'	9
2 Demanding a constitutional system of government	14
3 The Imo (Jingo) and Kapsin (Kōshin) Incidents – 'Empire' once again	25
4 The Sino-Japanese War: The birth of 'Empire' and the continuation of 'Constitution'	37

Part II The division between 'Empire' and 'Constitution'

Introduction: The system of apportionment between peace and democracy	53
5 Strong army and war weariness: 'Empire' and 'Constitution' before the Russo-Japanese War	57
6 From the Russo-Japanese War to the First World War: Struggle between 'Empire' and 'Constitution'	63
7 From the Taishō Political Change to the Siemens Affair: Stagnation of 'Empire' and Surge of 'Constitution'	84
8 The twenty-one demands to China: 'Constitution' domestically, 'Empire' externally	101

Part III The End of 'Constitution' and 'Empire'

Introduction: Japan between the two wars	115
9 What happened between the two world wars?	116
10 Three episodes between the two world wars	131
Conclusion: Irresponsible 'Empire' without 'Constitution'	149
Notes	161
Index	167

Introduction[1]

Japan was virtually a closed country during the Tokugawa Shogunate that lasted from the early seventeenth century until the so-called Meiji Restoration of 1868, whereby sovereignty was restored to the ancient line of emperors, thus replacing the military Shoguns that had displaced the emperors centuries before. Following the gradual opening of Japan to the outside world in the 1850s and 1860s, the country made spectacular progress towards the establishment of a modern state, capable of interacting with the major powers of Europe and North America on equal terms. This involved moving forward on a wide range of fronts, including the economy, law, education, politics and the development of modern armed forces.

The purpose of this book is to examine the inter-relationship between two crucial themes that guided the ambitions of various political and military leaders. These two themes I shall call 'Empire' and 'Constitution'. By 'Empire' I mean the drive to create colonies, on the models pioneered by most of the major world powers of the time. By 'Constitution' I mean the establishment of constitutional government, to provide stable regulation of the affairs of state. This was not the same thing as democracy, but it might contain elements of democracy. Whereas it has often been argued that the push for 'Empire' and the push for 'Constitution' were mutually opposed, I shall argue that the relationship between them was much more complex, at times involving symbiosis and at other times opposition, as well as mixtures of the two.

Beginning with 'Empire', Japan first began to make inroads into foreign countries in search of territory and special concessions in the Taiwan expedition of 1874. What it wished to obtain was the Ryūkyūs (present-day Okinawa), but the expedition targeted the Chinese territory of Taiwan. So far as 'Constitution' is concerned, the first real step taken by Japan towards introducing constitutional government began with the 'Edict to Establish a Constitutional Regime' proclaimed by the Meiji Emperor the following year, 1875. If the first was a move towards imperialism and the second a move towards constitutionalism, then in more than sixty years between then and the outbreak of the full-scale war between Japan and China in July 1937 both imperialism and constitutionalism made steady advances.

From a contemporary perspective, 'Empire' (colonization) is widely deplored, whereas 'Constitution' is regarded as attractive. But how should we best understand these two projects that seem so contradictory to us today – things that the Japanese, pulling together, created in a very short space of time? In the last year of the Meiji era (1912), the shameful expression 'Constitution at home, empire abroad' came into common usage. As this expression suggests, the view that this was an age where an expansionist policy abroad and constitutionalism at home did not contradict each other, was becoming widespread. But was this understanding really correct?

The present author has highlighted his personal expectation that with the advance of constitutionalism imperialism would decline. As this book will make clear, this expectation may be said to have been fulfilled. As a result of researching these two concepts over roughly a sixty-year period of Japanese modern history, it seems that while Constitution was progressing, Empire was being restrained.

Even so, though there were periods when Empire was retreating, it also went through phases where it was advancing. In essence this reminds us of the ceremony of beating the ground to chase the moles away, often seen in ancient times when someone was approaching an inn at a journey's final stage.

It is easy to say that when the forces of Constitution enter a pause, Empire gains in strength, but there were several instances where the exact opposite of this took place. Sometimes, when in the face of an adversary's military strength or popular opposition against Japan, Empire was compelled to hold its fire, and the forces of Constitution got their breath back.

More than seventy years have now elapsed since the end of the war, and during this period the Japanese have proclaimed their opposition to war. They have always had in mind 'our last great war', in other words the war against the United States between the end of 1941 and August 1945. But in the 67 years between 1874 and 1941, the targets of expanding military strength were always Korea and China, and with the sole exception of the Russo-Japanese war from 1904 to 1905, the adversary was always China.

This is abundantly evident when we consider the Taiwan expedition of 1874, the Sino-Japanese War of 1894, the twenty-one demands made against China in 1915, the Manchurian Incident of 1931 and the Marco Polo Bridge Incident of 1937. For completeness it is worth adding that while the war between Japan and the United States, which virtually all Japanese are aware of, was being fought, a war between Japan and China was also continuing. During all the periods in which Japanese imperialism was progressing, starting in 1874 and ending in 1945, Japan and China were continuously at loggerheads.

If we confine our investigation to the period before an all-out war was launched in 1937, efforts to promote constitutionalism domestically continued in parallel with it. If we look at the broad picture, there were phases, as I have pointed out, when Empire and Constitution got out of step with each other, but even so, 'Constitution' progressed, albeit at a slow pace. This seems clear if we list the following episodes: the Imperial Edict of 1875 establishing a constitutional regime; the movement in the 1880s to establish a national Parliament; the first constitutional defence movement in 1912–13; the universal male suffrage law of 1925; the system of two major political parties between 1925 and 1932; and the successes of legal Socialist Parties in the two general elections of 1936 and 1937.

The question is: What is the relationship of cause and effect between the two? There was in fact no overlap between periods of progress towards Empire and periods of progress towards the Constitution. The two periods did not interlink with each other. This was a happy discovery. The expression 'In domestic policy Constitution, in foreign policy Empire' does not stand up to scrutiny in the context of actual politics.

It follows that examples where Constitution and Empire were diametrically opposed were confined to a minority of instances. On the other hand, examples where imperialism completely overcame domestic constitutionalism were also not very common. Rather than continuous clashes between the two, there were relatively frequent examples of rotation between them.

*

I embarked on writing this book desirous of re-examining the truth or otherwise of the slogan 'in domestic policy Constitution, in foreign policy Empire', and thus the implication that constitutionalism failed in its attempts to check imperialism. That is why I use Empire and Constitution as equivalent concepts. In this book, which examines Japan–China relations largely as foreign relations, the use of 'imperialism' in modern historical research is inappropriate as a term to describe the foreign expansion of a highly advanced capitalist state. But pre-war Japan, which expanded its territory and special concessions in the Ryūkyūs, Taiwan, Korea, Manchuria and northern China, undoubtedly it was aiming at Empire.

I use the word 'Constitution' as a pair of characters (*rik ken*), as I explain in my argument, in a different sense from 'constitutionalism' (*rik ken shu gi*). The meaning of 'constitutionalism' (*rikkenshugi*) used in the post-war Constitution is to prevent the government of the day from misappropriating power. In pre-war Japan, by contrast, under the Constitution of the Great Japanese Empire (the Meiji Constitution), it was impossible to prevent misappropriation of power.

For instance, according to article 11 of the Constitution of the Great Japanese Empire, promulgated in 1889, 'The Emperor has supreme command of the Army and Navy'. 'Supreme command' meant the right to give directives and orders concerning military tactics and strategy. This was used as backing for the High Command of the army and navy (General Staff Office, Naval Command Office), and was interpreted to mean that the government (cabinet) was not allowed to interfere. This was the famous 'Independence of the Supreme Command'. As I shall discuss in detail throughout this book, in accordance with the Meiji Constitution, not only misappropriation of power but also reckless behaviour by the army and navy could not be prevented.

Discussion emerged about how to inhibit out-of-control behaviour by the military. Such discussion was 'pro-constitution' (*gōken*) but was 'not constitutionalism' (*hirikken*). The difference between *gōken* and *rikken* was spelled out by the democrat Yoshino Sakuzō. In a paper published in 1922, Yoshino set out the problem in the following way:

> The General Staff Office and the Naval Command Office in institutional terms already clearly clash with the duty of ministers of state to give assistance (in national administration the cabinet gives assistance to the Emperor). It goes without saying that this runs counter to the basic principles of the Constitution. Nevertheless, if we ask whether this represents a breach of the Constitution, we have to look at it to some extent in conjunction with other points of view.[2]

In taking this position, Yoshino indicated the limits to arguments put forward by the liberal constitutional scholar Minobe Tatsukichi. However much the Constitution of the Great Japanese Empire, so favourable to the military, were given a liberal interpretation, there was no way of modifying the provision that 'The Emperor has Supreme Command of the Army and Navy'. The freedom from control enjoyed by the central command of the army and navy was in conformity with the Constitution (*gōken*). In pre-war Japan, constitutionalism in the sense of 'constitutional limits on power' failed to prevent reckless behaviour by the military. In order to transcend and control the limits embodied in the Constitution of the Great Japanese Empire, Yoshino argued that what was needed was not constitutional exegesis, but return to the Basic Principles of the Constitution. In this book it is not 'Constitutionalism' (*rikkenshugi*), but 'Constitution' (*rikken*) that will be used in contraposition to 'Empire'. In this there is a hint of Yoshino's 'Basic Principles of the Constitution'.

And so, how can the Basic Principles of the Constitution transcend the Constitution's actual text? For Yoshino, who supported universal male suffrage, if that could be enacted, then through the power of a party cabinet based on a House of Representatives supported by all the people (not by constitutional interpretation but by the force of democracy), it would be possible to curb the excesses of the High Command.

In fact, just as Yoshino expected, cabinets of the *Rikken Minseitō* Party, led by Hamaguchi Osachi and Wakatsuki Reijirō, later gained absolute majorities in the House of Representatives under universal male suffrage. In both the London Naval Disarmament Treaty and in relation to the Manchurian Incident, they attempted to mount a degree of resistance against the demands and actions of the High Command. The Principles of Constitution continued to oppose Empire. But disputes between Empire and Constitution could not be extinguished with the establishment of universal suffrage and the custom (not the system) of party cabinets.[3] In pre-war Japan the struggle between the two was not resolved until the outbreak of an all-out war in the shape of the Pacific War. With the start of the Pacific War 'Constitution' was defeated, and with the defeat of Japan in that war, 'Empire' was also defeated.

The history of conflict between Empire, which began with the Taiwan expedition in 1874, and Constitution, which began with the Imperial Rescript of 1875, eventually arrived at this unhappy conclusion. But even so, or if it is really the case, what are the lessons that we should learn from it? In Japanese modern history, what was the nature of the conflict between Empire and Constitution? I shall examine this in detail in what follows.

Part I

The beginnings of 'Empire' and 'Constitution'

1842–95

1842	China defeated in Opium War (1840–).
1853	Commodore Perry and his fleet arrive in Uraga Bay.
1868	Proclamation of restored Imperial Rule. Toba Fushimi struggle (Boshin War, to 1869). Era name changed to Meiji. Charter Oath of five articles.
1871	Establishment of Imperial Armed Forces. Abolition of domains, replacement by prefectures. Japan–China Treaty of Friendship. Iwakura Mission embarks.
1872	Restructuring of Imperial Guard (Konoe force).
1873	Conscription edict. Land tax reform law. Split over argument whether to invade Korea (five councillors including Saigō Takamori resign).
1874	Petition to create an elected assembly. Ōkubo Toshimichi decides to send expedition to Taiwan. Saigō sets up private school in Kagoshima. Mutual provision between China and Japan.
1875	Ōsaka Conference (Ōkubo, Itagaki Taisuke, Kido Kōin). Taiwan expedition decided. Founding of Aikokusha. Council of Elders (Genrōin) established. Decree establishing constitutional system. Kangwhado Incident.
1876	Kangwhado Treaty (Japan–Korea Friendship Agreement).
1877	Land tax reduction (towards 2.5 per cent of land value). Seinan War.
1878	Ōkubo assassinated.
1879	Ryūkyū domain abolished. Okinawa prefecture established.
1880	League to establish a Parliament (Kokkai kisei dōmei). China threat argument of Yamagata Aritomo ('War preparations against neighbouring countries'). Army and navy build-up begins.
1881	Ōkuma Shigenobu: draft of new constitution and Parliament. Kōjunsha proposes private constitution. Inoue Kowashi: 'Opinion on a constitution.' Ueki Emori: 'Draft of a Japanese constitution.' Meiji political change (Ōkuma resigns). Imperial edict establishing a constitution. Jiyūtō founded.

1882 Matsukata deflation begins. Itō Hirobumi travels to Europe to research constitutions. Rikken Kaishintō founded. Imo (Jingo) Incident in Korea.
1884 Kapsin (Kōshin) Incident in Korea.
1885 Tientsin Treaty (both Japan and China to withdraw forces from Korea). Cabinet system launched.
1886 Naval loan floated.
1887 Inoue's 'Draft Constitution' sent to Prime Minister Itō.
1888 Privy Council (Sūmitsuin) established.
1890 First general elections. Imperial Diet begins.
1892 Second general elections (electoral interference on orders of Interior Minister Shinagawa).
1893 Imperial edict on harmony (edict on harmonious cooperation).
1894 Uprising by Tonghak Party in Korea. Sino-Japanese War.
1895 Shimonoseki Peace Conference. Signature of Shimonoseki Treaty. Triple intervention by Russia, Germany and France. Subjugation of Taiwan.

1

Defeating China – towards a 'small empire'

Split in the new Meiji government

The Taiwan expedition of 1874, and the increased tensions in Japan–China relations that followed it, was the most severe political crisis at the beginning of the Meiji era. The Japanese Army and Navy sent troops to Taiwan, which was Chinese territory, and with Chinese reactions a genuine fighting war was in prospect. This was six years after the restoration of the monarchy, and a mere three years since the greatest upheaval in modern Japanese history, namely the replacement of domains by prefectures.

At that time Kuroda Kiyotaka, who came from the Satsuma domain and as a councillor had been director of the Hokkaidō Development Office, was a hard-line advocate of war with China. At the same time he fully understood that Japanese military strength was insufficient. In a statement of opinion sent to Sanjō Sanetomi, the chief minister, and leading government official, Kuroda argued as follows:

> The key to waging war is for our Navy to be at the peak of its efficiency and to attack their Navy, destroy their ports and open a road for the Army to attack. In addition to a mere ten warships with which to carry out our duties, it is essential that we marshal a supplementary fleet. In Japan today there are about a hundred steamers belonging to various ministries, to the Hokkaidō Development Authority and in private hands. From these we should be able to choose the most robust vessels, and create a supplementary fleet of about 20 ships.

As is well known, after the arrival of Commodore Perry's fleet in 1853, the central point of naval policy was to import naval vessels and learn how to sail them. However, between the Restoration of 1868 and the Taiwan expedition of 1874 six years later, the Meiji government was battered by upheavals and by the civil war that they brought about. The army was strengthened by the civil war (Boshin War), but expansion of the navy had not yet been attempted. In other words, the first experience of international tension experienced by the Japanese government after the Restoration was the Taiwan expedition.

It was not only warships that were insufficient in number for the conduct of war. Internal political unity was also not enough. The Meiji government – which had overthrown the Bakufu in 1873, the year before the Taiwan expedition, without a basic line of policy being established – became seriously divided. The political upheaval of October 1873, well known as the 'split over subduing Korea', was a division among the three 'revolutionary domains' of Satsuma, Chōshū and Tosa. The Saigō Takamori group from the former Satsuma domain and the Itagaki Taisuke group from the former Tosa domain left the government.

At that time Saigō and others, who had been advocating a positive approach towards Korea, came out against the 'subdue Korea' argument. Even in the Chōshū group that supported Ōkubo Toshimichi's advocacy of giving priority to domestic affairs, the representative of that position, Kido Kōin, left the government, since the Taiwan expedition would run counter to a domestic priority policy. Even Yamagata Aritomo, the doyen of the military in the same faction, who remained within the government, totally opposed the Taiwan expedition on the grounds that it would lead to war with China. In July 1874, before the cabinet decision that did not reject the possibility of war with China, Yamagata sent the following statement of opinion to the government:

> In Japan today officers are insufficiently trained, and soldiers have not received enough instruction. Stockpiles of weapons are also insufficient. Even if we prevail in fighting on Taiwan, which is small in population and land area, the consequences will be incalculable if it precipitates war with China.

Over the forty-eight years between then and his death in 1922, Yamagata consistently warned against underestimating China. Sixty years after the Taiwan expedition, at a time when war between Japan and China was continuing to spread, Tōyama Mitsuru, who had been the central figure among right-wing Asianists, stated bitterly that if Yamagata were still alive, the current mess would probably have been averted.[1] Former Asianists such as Tōyama Mitsuru and Ogawa Heikichi (see the final chapter for further discussion), who argued for the defence of Asia against aggression by the Great Powers, would have happily supported it if Great Britain were attacked to defend China. But they absolutely could not understand the demands of nationalists after the Japan–China War for a war against Britain in order to attack China.

Kuroda of Satsuma, who together with Ōkubo Toshimichi and Saigō Takamori had promoted revolution against the Shogunate and engineered the

Meiji Restoration, did not believe that it would be possible to fight a war against China while the government was split. He strongly argued that naval strength needed to be augmented, and that the Meiji government should revert to the situation it was in before it split. Kuroda, preparing for war with China, argued in favour of establishing an Imperial headquarters, of bringing together Saigō, Kido and Itagaki, all of whom were out of government, and tried to persuade the government that an all-Japan system should be set up, as follows:

> His Majesty the Emperor should himself control military affairs (as Chief of the General Staff) proclaim his personal decree, and unify the direction of the whole people. It is the duty of the Chief of the General Staff to fulfil the Imperial Will, and control the military. Sanjō, the Prime Minister, should take care of this.
>
> It is urgent and important to assist the Chief of the General Staff, keep the whole army together, and plan methods of attack. When a cease-fire is decided, an emissary of the Emperor should be sent urgently, Army General Saigō, Councillor Kido and former Councillor Itagaki should be despatched to Kyoto, Councillors Yamagata Aritomo (still serving) and Ijichi Masaharu should be added to them, a High Command should be established, and strategy should be discussed as a priority.[2]

Saigō, Itagaki and Kido, mentioned earlier, are all famous in Japan, but Ijichi Masaharu is relatively unknown. In fact he was a figure who led the royalists in the Satsuma domain, and his special area of expertise was military strategy. It was Ijichi who directed the Boshin War on the spot in 1868 following the overthrow of the Bakufu by force. Naturally he joined the High Command together with Yamagata who came from Chōshū.

The Japan–China confrontation over Ryūkyū – the Taiwan expedition

The aim, however, of the Taiwan expedition, which took place just before the Japan–China War broke out, was to force China to recognize Japan's sovereignty over the Ryūkyūs (Okinawa). The Japanese side wished to complete its pursuit of Chinese responsibility for the assassination just three years earlier in November 1871 of forty-five Ryūkyūan fishermen who had drifted onto the shores of Taiwan. The Chinese government, however, would not agree to this. The reason was clear, namely that 'We are aware that on our territory of Taiwan fishermen from our tributary territory of Ryūkyū were assassinated, but we have not heard of *Japanese fishermen* being killed'. When they received this reply, the Japanese side responded that if the Chinese government rejected its own responsibility, they would themselves punish the culprits. This was the reason for the expedition.

Within the Meiji government, it was primarily the former Satsuma elements that were positive about military action. Apart from Kuroda Kiyotaka, the naval deputy secretary Kawamura Sumiyoshi and the army deputy secretary Saigō Tsugumichi constituted the hard-line faction, and in the 'subdue Korea' dispute the Army General Saigō Takamori resigned as councillor, gathered samurai elements from Kagoshima and supported the expedition. As a result, in May 1874, the expedition was put into action. It was a large-scale force, consisting of four warships and naval and army personnel. In addition, although the numbers in the volunteer force under Saigō's command is unknown, since 3,500 troops are said to have landed on Taiwan, if we deduct the 3,000 regular troops we are left with 500 as a likely total.

Ōkubo Toshimichi's peace negotiations

In international terms, the arbitrary designation of Ryūkyūans, whose nationality was not agreed between Japan and China, as Japanese citizens, and the despatch of a naval and military expedition to Taiwan, which was Chinese territory, constituted aggression. The Chinese government demanded immediate and unconditional withdrawal of the Japanese troops, and Western powers, including Britain, supported the Chinese assertions. But as we have already noted, former Satsuma domain elements controlled the Japanese government, and they were prepared to go to war with China. So long as there was no powerful politician from Satsuma aiming to resolve the situation, a full-scale war between Japan and China would be difficult to avoid.

The man who was willing to take onto himself the dissatisfactions of the hard-line faction was the councillor and home minister, Ōkubo Toshimichi. It was he who, together with Saigō Takamori leading the Satsuma domain, brought about the Meiji Restoration.

Ōkubo, who arrived in Peking as ambassador plenipotentiary of the Japanese government, from 14 September 1874 began negotiations with China. Discussions lasted over seven sessions until 23 October, but no compromise between the two sides was reached, and the situation was on the verge of breakdown. Ōkubo announced the ending of negotiations, since the Japanese government was unable to agree with the Chinese claim that Taiwan was under its own jurisdiction.

But Ōkubo, from the time of the fourth discussion session, was attempting to find grounds for compromise behind the scenes. The Japanese side withdrew their insistence that Taiwan was outside Chinese jurisdiction, but instead argued that since it was within Chinese jurisdiction, China bore responsibility for the events concerned. As well as presenting this compromise proposal, on the 23rd he announced the breakdown of negotiations.

The Chinese side too understood Ōkubo's message. Through the good offices of the British minister, Wade, a compatibility clause between Japan and China was proposed (and signed on 31 October). It consisted of three points:

1. Without reference to the status of Ryūkyū, China acknowledges that the present Taiwan expedition was for a 'noble humanitarian purpose'.
2. For the Japanese casualties in the expedition, the Chinese government will pay 500,000 taels, not as 'reparations' but as 'relief aid'. Since China will have the use of facilities built by Japan during the expedition, the Chinese side will pay their expenses.
3. Henceforth the Chinese government will take responsibility for security on Taiwan, and guarantees the safety of travellers.

Ōkubo as plenipotentiary put his seal on this clause. Of course, since he knew that his own government and the Kagoshima samurai class had prepared for war against China in all seriousness, he expected a fair degree of dissatisfaction with the clause. But if he was to take responsibility of the State and the people, there was no choice apart from affixing his seal.

As I have already pointed out, since Ryūkyū was not under formal Japanese jurisdiction, and Japan sent an expeditionary force to Taiwan which was under Chinese jurisdiction, this flew in the face of international norms. Nevertheless, the Chinese government accepted it as a 'noble humanitarian act', and did not treat it as 'wrong'. In addition, against clear Chinese strategy, China, though refusing to pay 'reparations', conceded that it should pay 'relief aid'. If Japan had ignored this and had embarked on a war with China, interference by the Western Great Powers could not have been avoided. Even if the matter were limited to Japan–China relations, as I have already noted, there was no guarantee of victory.

Ōkubo Toshimichi, well understanding his unpopularity at home, put an end to the reckless Taiwan expedition, and at the end of November 1874 returned to Japan.

2

Demanding a constitutional system of government

The Ōsaka Conference

Between the Japan–China confrontation in 1874 and the second confrontation, to be described in Chapter 3, lay the 'constitution period'.

The very first example of 'Constitution' being proposed with the clear intention of forestalling 'Empire' is known in Japanese modern history as the 'Ōsaka Conference'. This was a meeting between Kido Kōin (former Chōshū domain samurai) and Itagaki Taisuke (former Tosa domain samurai).

In fact, what was famous about the Ōsaka Conference was that on 11 February 1875, it became a three-man meeting with the addition of Ōkubo Toshimichi (former Satsuma domain samurai). However, from this book's position of counterposing Empire with Constitution, it is the 'Ōsaka Conference' on 22 January between the constitutionalist Kido, and Itagaki, who supported a popularly elected House, that deserves greater significance.

The meeting on that day was arranged through negotiations between Inoue Kaoru of the former Chōshū domain, Furusawa Shigeru of the former Tosa domain and Komuro Shinobu of the former Tokushima domain. It is worth noting that these three men met for the first time the very next day (28 November 1874) once Ōkubo Toshimichi had returned to the port of Yokohama after dealing with the aftermath of the Taiwan expedition in Peking. Very soon after Ōkubo returned home after concluding his very difficult negotiations with the Chinese side, which was angry about the Taiwan expedition, the movement in favour of 'Constitution' rather than of 'Empire' became energized.

Inoue Kaoru, in a letter written three days later on 1 December, reported to Kido Kōin about the three-man meeting held on 28 November. This letter is important in that it demonstrates the relationship between 'Empire' and 'Constitution'.

In the letter to Kido, Inoue asked him to order his subordinates Itō Hirobumi and Yamagata Aritomo, 'not to act in such a way as to foment other wars', but rather to take care to cut excess expenditure, and concentrate on the slogans: 'prosperous nation, strong army' (*fukoku kyōhei*) as well as 'civilization and enlightenment'(*bunmei kaika*)* This constituted a check on 'Empire'.

Following this, Inoue reported that he had met Furusawa and Komuro Shinobu, who had drafted the 'White paper on establishing a popularly elected parliament' on the ship en route for Ōsaka. Inoue sought to achieve a compromise between Kido, who was one of those who had spent over a year as part of the Iwakura Mission refining his ideas while investigating Europe and America to produce a German-style constitutional plan, and Furusawa together with Komuro, who in the same period studied in Britain and favoured a parliamentary system. The three men agreed that while Inoue would invite Kido to Ōsaka, Furusawa and Komuro would persuade Itagaki to come to Ōsaka, thus having the two leading participants enter into discussion with each other.

In a letter that Inoue sent again to Kido on 18 December, he urged that 'a compromise be arrived at between your argument and that of Itagaki, and a parliament should be established appropriate for Japanese characteristics, with sufficient power granted to government'.[1] He was against the British model supported by Itagaki, based on an elected Parliament, but believed that the German model, with a strong executive, should be adopted; however that might be, a compromise between the two factions should, in his opinion, be worked out.

It seems clear that if we put together the proposal to set up a Parliament and the desire, noted earlier, to eliminate the possibility of another war with Korea, then establishing a Parliament ('Constitution') and avoiding war with Korea and China should be regarded as all of a piece. Based on these preparations, the meeting was held on 11 February 1875. The situation on that day is made clear by Kido's diary:

> At eleven in the morning Inoue arrived at my hotel, and from after one o'clock we visited Itagaki's place together. Komuro and Furusawa were there as well. We gave our opinion on their proposal to set up a popular assembly, heard their ideas, and at about eight o'clock we went to Inoue's house, where the two of us went into more detail on these topics.[2]

This five-man meeting between Itagaki, Komuro, Furusawa, Kido and Inoue took place over seven hours between one o'clock in the afternoon and eight o'clock in the evening.

---

* Translator's note: These became key government slogans during the Meiji period.

The Imperial Edict establishing a constitutional structure

The results of this meeting were transmitted by Kido to Ōkubo Toshimichi, and consequently, on 11 February, a three-man meeting took place between Ōkubo, Kido and Itagaki, known as the 'Ōsaka Conference'. What converted the results of this three-man conference into a formal resolution of the Meiji government was the 'Imperial Edict to establish a Constitutional Regime' on 14 April 1875, regarded by the present writer as the starting point for Meiji constitutionalism. Given that it was a crucial edict marking a transition from Empire to Constitution, I reproduce it below in its original form, though modernizing its spelling and punctuation.

> After we came to the throne, and met many people, we swore an oath of five articles [the Imperial Oath of five articles, or Charter Oath], we determined national policy and set a path to safeguard the integrity of the whole population.... We now wish to expand the content of the Oath, by establishing an Assembly of Elders [*genrōin*], thus broadening the source of legislation, put the legislative function firmly in place by establishing a Deliberative Assembly (*daishin'in*), and also through assembling local officials to pursue the public good, *gradually establishing a constitutional State*, so that together with you our subjects, we wish to enjoy the fruits of these reforms[3] [author's italics].

The fact that in April 1875, only eight years after the Meiji Restoration, the Meiji Emperor should have promised that he would 'gradually establish a constitutional State' was of the greatest importance. But in this book, whose task is to investigate the relationship between Empire and Constitution, it is crucial to recognize that the first step towards the Imperial Edict was taken on the day after Ōkubo Toshimichi, who had managed to calm tensions in relations between Japan and China precipitated by the Taiwan expedition, disembarked at the port of Yokohama. In order to contain 'Empire', the first step towards 'Constitution' was taken.

The Edict establishing a Parliament: Ending of the constitution-building period

If I am correct in my historical explanation, once the 'constitution period' that began at the end of 1874 came to an end, a new 'Empire' period would begin.

As will be elucidated in the next chapter, the next confrontation between Japan and China occurred in July 1882. About nine months earlier, in October 1881, the leading disciples of Ōkuma Shigenobu and Fukuzawa Yukichi were expelled from the Meiji government (the 1881 political upheaval). This is famous as the upheaval that heralded the defeat of the Popular Rights Movement.

On 12 October, two days after the upheaval on the tenth, the Imperial Edict proclaiming 'the ending of the constitutional period' was announced. I shall explain later the reason why this Edict, announcing that the Diet (Parliament) would be inaugurated nine years later in 1890, was interpreted as heralding 'the ending of the constitutional period', but I will now cite just the most important part of the edict:

> Our intention is that in 1890 Diet members will assemble and the Diet will be inaugurated. We have ordered Government officials to take responsibility for planning this with due despatch.[4]

As we have already explained, the Imperial Edict of 1875 promised 'gradually to establish a constitutional State'. And then more than six years elapsed until October 1881, but as for 'gradually', it went on for another nine years, making a total of fifteen. In contemporary politics the word 'postponement' is used a great deal. But a fifteen-year postponement is something else altogether. This was one reason for identifying the 1881 Edict as proclaiming 'the end of constitutionalism'.

From the Kanghwado Incident to the Popular Rights Movement

If the 1875 Edict was 'the beginning of the constitutional period', and the Edict of 1881 was 'The ending of the constitutional period', the six years between the two of them were surely 'the constitution period'. But to encompass the six years in this way is not how the matter is generally understood.

For instance, on 20 September 1875 the Kanghwado (Japanese Kōkadō) Incident erupted in Korea. This seems to have been an armed demonstration on the part of the Japanese side, used against Korea, which was trying to reject the signature of a trade treaty, and we may say that it was putting flesh on the idea of subduing Korea.

In the meantime a whole series of events took place, including the takeover of government by Ōkubo Toshimichi and Ōkuma Shigenobu, who were promoting industrialization from above, a series of 'samurai revolts', typified by the Saigō Takamori upheaval (the Seinan war), attempts to bring about 'development dictatorship', mainly promoted by Ōkubo as home minister, and the assassination of Ōkubo that followed. Passing through this period of instability, finally by

1879 the 'Constitution' group came to the fore. All over the country popular rights associations, such as the Aikokusha (Patriotic Society), were formed, culminating in the 1880 congress of the Kokkai kisei dōmei (League for the Establishment of a National Assembly), so that the three-year period from 1879 to 1881 was when the 'Popular Rights Movement period' was at its most active.

But even though various events took place in the meantime there was a consistent trend towards 'Constitution' over the six years from 1875. Within the 'Constitution faction', relations between radicals and moderates did not show much variation, and apart from the Kangwhado Incident in September 1875, forces seeking to move towards 'Empire' were kept under control. Moreover, one of the central personalities in the moderate faction was Inoue Kaoru, while the top man in the radical faction was Itagaki Taisuke, as he had been six years earlier. The so-called Popular Rights Movement is best understood as an extension of the Ōsaka Conference of 1875.

The radical faction movement centred on Itagaki Taisuke reached its peak at the Congress of the League for the Establishment of a National Assembly in March 1880. In the 'White Paper on establishing a Popular Assembly' all of the eight who signed it were of samurai origin, but among the ninety-seven representatives of societies from various regions who signed a document petitioning the Emperor to establish a Parliament – a proposal adopted at the conference of March 1880 – sixty-one were of samurai origin, and thirty-six were commoners, many being wealthy farmers who had been added. Despite this change, however, the core of the movement remained the Aikokusha led by Itagaki, and this had not changed.

Miscalculation by Inoue Kaoru

Between 1874 and 1875 Inoue Kaoru – at the centre of the argument within the moderate faction about setting up a Parliament, after working hard to finalize a treaty of friendship between Japan and Korea (the Kangwhado Treaty) – went to London to research the political and economic situation. But when he learned of the assassination of the Home Minister Ōkubo Toshimichi in May 1878, he immediately made preparations to return home. Arriving back in Japan in July, he made a comeback as a central figure in the government, as State Councillor and Minister for Industry. Inoue, during his stay in London, became more closely acquainted with the disciples of Fukuzawa Yukichi. The visibility of Inoue as a high official of the Japanese government despatched on missions means that he must have lived in a large house. He held a study group every Saturday at his home, where he invited Nakamigawa Hikojirō, Koizumi Nobukichi and other disciples of Fukuzawa.

An important point about this study group is that both Inoue and Fukuzawa's disciples felt more strongly that they should not be too much hoodwinked by the 'popular assembly argument' of Itagaki and others presented at the time of the Ōsaka Conference earlier on. At the end of 1880, when Inoue was becoming politically active again, through Fukuzawa he seems to have placed great store on the Kōjunsha. This was a social club of about 1,700 members, mainly graduates of Keiō Gijuku University, which Fukuzawa had founded. It included men in commerce and industry, journalists and university teachers. Inoue had no intention of establishing contact with Itagaki, who was working to set up a Parliament, on which he held two conferences in 1880.

Inoue, however, seems to have overestimated the conservatism of political thought influenced by Fukuzawa. In a letter of October 1876 to Kido Kōin, who remained in Japan while Inoue was in London interacting with Fukuzawa's disciples, Inoue wrote in general terms about their mode of thinking:

> I am staying with Fukuzawa's three students here, and studying their behaviour has been a useful learning process. Their character is outstanding. While they were in Japan they were just calling for 'freedom' in an abstract manner, but recently they have substantially repented, and become 'conservative' [in English in the text]. They have now come to realise that such things as a popularly elected assembly will be most difficult to realise, and they have begun to assert that unless a country acts 'practically', it will be not be able to increase national 'wealth', which is the most important factor. They meet every Saturday at my house to discuss books on economics ('political economy'), arguing about them in the context of Japanese conditions, and they derive great benefit from this. People who aspire to genuine learning, people who have real patriotic feeling, gradually become *consorubeechibu* (conservative), something that is most attractive. I am becoming more and more convinced that it is not a good idea to be radical.[5]

Even among the letters of Meiji period leaders Inoue's were rich in content, but contained rather frequent non-sequiturs. Moreover this letter, written while he was in London, contained many English words rendered in Japanese *katakana* script. In addition, even though he put words into 'katakana English', in the case of 'conservative', he revealed that his English was quite theoretical.

Quite apart from the fact that he was 'processing' words in this way, we need to examine Inoue's concept of a duality between 'conservative' and 'radical'. I have been arguing that the history of pre-war Japan cannot be understood using a bipolar distinction between 'conservative' and 'radical', and that a three-way division of 'conservative', 'moderate' and 'radical' is what is needed. For Inoue around 1880, however, it was only the two-way distinction that made sense. I think that whether the political outlook of a particular politician is bipolar or tripolar means little in terms of historical development. But Inoue, throughout the Bakumatsu and Restoration periods, was one of the central figures in the powerful Chōshū domain, as well as in the 'post-Restoration' Chōshū domain faction (after the domains had been abolished). He was also a key adviser to the Emperor during the writing of the Imperial Edict of April 1875, mentioned earlier. If *Inoue*'s bipolar framework were mistaken, this would be a far cry from the views of a mere student of history such as the present writer, and would have decisively influenced the fate of Meiji constitutionalism.

As I have already pointed out more than once in this book, Fukuzawa Yukichi and the Kōjunsha that he directed were moderate liberals, aiming to establish a British-style parliamentary cabinet system, and were not 'conservatives'. In his 1879 work *Minjō isshin* (Radical Change in People's Way of Thinking), he used as a model British politics, where 'conservatism' that is open-minded, and 'radicalism' of a kind that avoids absurd proposals for reform, alternate in power every four or five years.

Seen, however, from a bipolar division between conservatives and radicals, Fukuzawa's argument may appear close to 'conservatism' at times. The radical popular rights activist Ueki Emori severely criticized Fukuzawa as a proponent of 'compromise between officials and the people'.

On the other hand, according to the ultra-conservative Minister of the Right Iwakura Tomomi, as well as Inoue Kowashi, Chief Secretary of the Dajōkan and others, Fukuzawa Yukichi and the Kōjunsha appeared closely linked with the popular rights faction. A letter sent in July 1881 by Inoue Kowashi to the Councillor Itō Hirobumi warned in the following terms that it was Fukuzawa and his Kōjunsha that were the control tower of the national movement to set up a Parliament:

> The fact that he who is petitioning for a parliament is not calling for it at present is not because he is silent. According to information arriving from many places, they have all shifted their focus to researching a constitution, and this constitutional research is only possible by relying on Fukuzawa's private draft constitution (or the Kōjunsha's private draft constitution). Because this is so, Fukuzawa's Kōjunsha is now putting out propaganda throughout the country, it is the biggest machine for influencing the birth of political parties, its power

is stealthily increasing, it penetrates the brain and ferments within it. Its promoters control a hundred thousand elite troops that possess the vigour to cross uninhabited plains.⁶

According to Inoue Kowashi, the movement to petition for a Parliament welled up in 1880 throughout the country; in 1881 it was taken out of the hands of Itagaki Taisuke, and placed under the influence of Fukuzawa Yukichi and the Kōjunsha. As I explain in my book *Meiji demokurashii* (*Meiji Democracy*) and elsewhere, Inoue's view on this matter exaggerated the role of Fukuzawa and the Kōjunsha. As before, the central figures in the democracy petition movement were Itagaki and his followers.

The issue, however, does not rest here. The current government was based on the former Satsuma and Chōshū domains that had played the central role in bringing about the Meiji Restoration. The problem is that conservatives within what was known as the 'domain-faction government' regarded Fukuzawa and the Kōjunsha as more dangerous than Itagaki and his followers. On the other hand, Inoue Kaoru (not Inoue Kowashi) had asked Fukuzawa for assistance in having the government set up a Parliament from above.

Broadly speaking, assuming that there was a right wing and a left wing within the domain-faction government, Inoue Kowashi was right wing and Inoue Kaoru was left wing. And if we investigate in the same way those calling for a Parliament to be established, Fukuzawa was right wing while Itagaki was left wing. Mutual affinity between those on the left wing of a rightist faction and those on the right wing of a radical faction is no doubt a political constant. Inoue Kaoru saw Fukuzawa as more conservative than he actually was, and Fukuzawa regarded Inoue as more progressive than he really was.

Fukuzawa Yukichi and Inoue Kaoru

The process of coming together and moving apart between these two men as a result of each overestimating the other can be appreciated from a letter that Fukuzawa sent to Inoue Kaoru and Itō Hirobumi immediately after the '1881 Political Change' resulting from it. The letter describes realistically, from Fukuzawa's position, the process of negotiation between the three progressive councillors of the Meiji government – Inoue Kaoru, Ōkuma Shigenobu and Itō Hirobumi, on the one hand, and Fukuzawa, representing the Kōjunsha, on the other. This takes up ten pages of the *Fukuzawa Yukichi zenshū* (*Collected Works* of *Fukuzawa Yukichi*, vol. 17, pp. 471–80). Unfortunately, the reader is asked to make do with the present writer's summary.

As I have already pointed out, Nakamigawa Hikojirō, when Inoue returned to Japan as foreign minister, became head of the Bureau for Official Communications under him in the same ministry. Nakamigawa was tasked to visit his respected teacher, Fukuzawa, and transmitted to him Inoue's request to take on responsibility for publication of government-line newspapers. When Fukuzawa replied that he would want to consider this after seeing some kind of prospectus of the publications as a whole, Inoue replied that it would be better to hold a meeting. As a result, on 24 or 25 December 1880, he met Councillor Ōkuma Shigenobu, following Nakamigawa's invitation, and Itō Hirobumi came also.

At Ōkuma's house, Ōkuma and Itō, harmonizing their views, requested Fukuzawa to assume responsibility for the newspapers, but Fukuzawa avoided a quick reply. After mature thought, he strengthened his determination 'firmly to refuse this request' if 'newspapers within the present government system fail to disseminate the government's real intentions for the sake of maintaining the cabinet as it is at present'. In January 1881, he visited the house of Inoue Kaoru, and reported as follows:

Inoue with a straight face says:

> Let me say directly that the government is prepared to set up a parliament. And I have no regrets at all about this. If any political party progresses sufficiently, I am prepared to yield government, as a perfectly normal matter, to those who have obtained popular support.

And then in addition, he says that Inoue told the following to Fukuzawa:

> Since everything has now been planned together with Itō and Ōkuma, and has been firmly contracted, nothing can be changed. In order to open up such a major issue, the three councillors will never betray Fukuzawa, and Fukuzawa should not deceive the three councillors.... If there is any doubt about this, you may meet with Ōkuma to confirm this. And then proof of it may be obtained. In all my life I have never before experienced so great a breach of promise.[7]

Fukuzawa seems to have been really glad to hear Inoue's discourse. Fukuzawa wrote: 'I didn't know your real intentions. Thus the happiness of the Meiji government means the eternity of Japan. . . . I also use my right arm for my country.' And he accepted the position of responsibility for government newspapers.

As is clear from this summary, Inoue promised Fukuzawa not just the establishment of a Parliament but also a parliamentary cabinet system. This is demonstrated by Inoue's statement: 'If any party progresses sufficiently to establish a cabinet, I am ready to yield government to those who have obtained popular support.' In Fukuzawa's casual remarks following his main discourse, Fukuzawa's memory shows that the two men came to the same conclusion concerning also a parliamentary cabinet system:

> Later we were chatting, imagining the state of affairs after a parliament was set up, how the parties were likely to be divided up, who the leaders would be, whether parties would capture government, whether so-and-so would become foreign minister, whether so-and-so would be home minister. If these things happened, would Inoue fall by the wayside, would he leave the chamber as a single member of parliament, or would he give a speech in the House as a former Foreign Minister? – these were the kinds of prospect we discussed, and it was really interesting.[8]

Alienation – postponing the establishment of a Parliament

Up to this point I have developed a fairly detailed introduction to discussions between Fukuzawa and Inoue. If we take this as our premise, it is reasonable to conclude that Fukuzawa and the Kōjunsha wanted to introduce a British-style system of cabinet within a Parliament, as well as a system based on two large parties, while Inoue Kaoru (who had spent about two years in London) was of the same opinion.

At the end of July 1881, however, around seven months later, Inoue sent a letter to his colleague, Itō Hirobumi, in which he argued as follows:

> Already today since the situation is urgent, and we must do something, we should quickly learn from the German Constitution, and make detailed studies of the German legal system. So we should urgently elect from among local members, and have it discuss the draft of a Constitution, submit the result to the Chamber of Elder Statesmen, and then after one or two years proclaim the opening of the lower house. . . .
>
> In fact the British political system is called a constitutional monarchy, but its essence, much more so than in the case of the American republican system, is only suitable for Great Britain and was constructed as a result of common law, which has little to teach other countries. Today among those engaged in Western studies, there are very many who study Great Britain or France, and for this reason they think that the British system is the best, but they do not understand that it cannot be transferred to other countries. Fukuzawa and others are like

this. Therefore, I believe that this is an excellent opportunity, not to be lost, for the rapid assimilation of German law.[9]

It was difficult to imagine that Inoue was the same person as the Inoue who, in a meeting with Fukuzawa seven months before, had been laughing with him and imagining himself as an opposition member as the result of a change of government, and as a former foreign minister attacking the government on foreign policy issues in the House of Representatives.

If, however, we consider the letter, mentioned earlier, which he sent to Kido Kōin from London in 1876, it is possible to say that it was precisely this position that represented Inoue's fundamental thinking. At that time five years before, he was writing: 'People who aspire to genuine learning, people who have genuine patriotic feeling, gradually become *consorubeechibu* [conservative], something that is most attractive. I am becoming more and more convinced that it is not a good idea to be radical.'

Meiji constitutionalism as perceived in this book began with the 1875 Imperial Edict, centred on Inoue Kaoru, who called himself conservative. What may be called a coup d'état (the 1881 Political Change) was carried out by the conservative faction within the Meiji government, in which Inoue Kaoru was one of the central figures. As a result of this, the curtain was lowered by issuing the 'Imperial Edict to Establish a Parliament' in October 1881. By this Imperial Edict the promulgation of a Parliament was postponed for nine years. This disappointing interruption was brought about because the conservative Inoue Kaoru and the moderate Fukuzawa Yukichi each over-assimilated the other's ideas. A year after the curtain came down on 'Constitution' (1882), with the Jingo (Japanese name), or Imo (Korean name) incident, 'Empire' period once again began.

3

The Imo (Jingo) and Kapsin (Kōshin) Incidents – 'Empire' once again

The China threat argument and the return of the 'strong army' argument

After the Taiwan expedition in 1874, which ended in a division of pain, Ch'ing Dynasty China, with Japan in mind, strove to expand and modernize its army and navy. The Japanese military authorities took note of this at the end of 1880. Yamagata Aritomo, the headquarters director (later commanding officer) of the High Command (at the time the army and navy command) presented to the Emperor a research report entitled 'Military Preparations and Strategy of Neighbouring Powers'. In a supplementary submission, there was a section on the 'Chinese threat', and on the need for Japan to shift its emphasis from a 'prosperous country' to a 'strong army'.

Yamagata first of all pointed out that Chinese territory and population were about ten times larger than those of Japan. The population of the two countries was about 400,000,000 in the case of China and 40,000,000 in the case of Japan. That is almost exactly the same proportion as it is today, 137 years later.

China, a great power with a population and land area ten times that of Japan, had expanded its military in both quality and size less than six years after the Japanese Taiwan expedition. Yamagata wrote that it had built huge shipbuilding works and was building more and more warships (it seemed unlikely that China at that period was building warships unaided), in many places it was establishing munitions factories, in important ports it was setting up batteries, and it was engaged in military training in both the British and German fashion.

For Yamagata, who was a supreme realist in military matters, and from that point of view as army minister six years earlier had argued against war with China, Chinese modernization and development as a major power was neither something to be complacent about, nor to rejoice in. Rather than subscribing to a model in which Japan and China should unite in confronting the great powers of Europe and America, he held that the situation was one of direct confrontation between the two countries as rivals. In his words: 'The remarkable military preparations of both these neighbouring countries are something to be both applauded and feared.' For Yamagata, who thought in this way, the policies that had prevailed since the Taiwan expedition under the Interior Minister Ōkubo Toshimichi needed to be amended. This meant amending the priority Ōkubo was giving to the slogan 'prosperous country', meaning promotion of investment and development of industry. He reversed the order of 'prosperous country' and 'strong army', arguing as follows:

> If the armed forces are strengthened, the morale of the people will be elevated, we may speak of freedom of the people, the people's rights may be discussed, foreign relations may be defended on the basis of equality, profit may be obtained from trade, the people's wealth may be defended. For many years 'prosperous country' and 'strong army' have had equal status.[1]

In the final phrase he places them on an equal footing, but it is clear from his article as a whole that 'strong army' is in first place.

Changing relationship between Japan and Korea, and advent of confrontation between Japan and China

In 1880 when the army and navy under Yamagata Aritomo, chief of the general staff office, had been insisting on the threat from China, the Foreign Ministry was planning to make relations between Japan and Korea more intimate. The Japanese side, by using military pressure to force open the ports of Wonsan and Incheon, as provided for in the Treaty of Friendship between Japan and Korea (the Kanghwado Treaty of 1876), seemed able to achieve this.

A big change, however, appeared on the Korean side. Whereas the conservatives held real power in Korea and were dependent on China, forces linked with Japan and the planning reform were emerging to prominence. In February 1881, about three months after Yamagata's petition to the Throne cited earlier, the Japanese minister in Korea, Hanabusa Yoshimoto, reported that those within Korea who planned rapprochement with Japan 'possess both learning and financial resources, have failed to achieve positions within government befitting their status, understand to some extent overseas structures, and wish to reform domestic Korean politics'.[2] Hanabusa's understanding was that in opposition to them, the current government, which was against commercial intercourse with Japan, consisted of very senior bureaucratic and military officials with an interest in protecting their own positions, dependent on China and maintaining anti-Japanese attitudes.

It is clear from this that if the Japanese government aimed to improve relations between Japan and Korea with the help of pro-Japan reformists, Japan–Korea relations would have an influence on relations between Japan and China since the conservatives had close relations with China. And China now had succeeded in modernizing its armed forces to an extent difficult to imagine from the perspective of the Taiwan expedition several years earlier.

The subtle 'Asianism' of Fukuzawa Yukichi: Underestimation of China

The situation that while China was becoming a strong country, Korea was divided internally between a pro-China faction and a pro-Japan faction, presented Japan with a rather difficult problem.

If the Meiji government and the press were to take a hard-nosed attitude towards China in the manner of Yamagata Aritomo, then rather than depending complacently on the rise of the pro-Japan faction in Korea, they should work to build up their military forces in order to match those of China. But among the Japanese leaders who were only concerned with foreign pressure from the great powers of Europe and America, there were substantial numbers who underestimated China.

Fukuzawa Yukichi, who was a leading advocate of assimilating Western civilization, was one of those.

In a lengthy pamphlet entitled *Jiji shōgen* (Some thoughts on Current Events), published in September 1881, shortly after a roughly sixty-member delegation centred on the pro-Japan reform faction had visited Japan, Fukuzawa argued in the following terms that China was unable to modernize rapidly as Japan had done:

> Even though the Chinese give the impression that they are trying to open up to some extent, this is merely one part in ten million, and they cannot easily exert influence to this end across the whole country. In order to implant modern civilisation into China, it would be necessary to reform the minds of Chinese people as a whole, otherwise they cannot engage in intensive training following the Japanese precedent.[3]

On the other hand, Fukuzawa welcomed the acceptance into Keiō Gijuku University of two Korean leaders who had been part of the delegation mentioned earlier. In a letter to his disciple Koizumi Shinkichi, he wrote as follows about this matter. Since it is a letter that reveals Fukuzawa's feelings accurately, I will reproduce it as close as possible to the original script:

> Early this month (June) a number of Koreans arrived to acquaint themselves with the state of affairs in Japan. Among them two young men have enrolled in our school, the two together have been staying in my house, and I have been readily encouraging them. When I think back to my own life over twenty years ago, I cannot refrain from thinking of them in compassionate terms. . . . with this as a beginning, Koreans of high and low status are frequently visiting my house, and when I start talking about this, it is just like Japan of thirty years ago. In future I want to cultivate good relations with them.[4]

In this he was bringing together the arrival in Japan of the two Koreans with his own journeys to America and Europe in 1860 and 1862, and what they told him about the situation in Korea compared with the arrival of Perry's fleet in Japan in 1853. The first of these was twenty years before, the second thirty years before.

As I noted earlier, Fukuzawa regarded Chinese modernization and the achievement of a 'prosperous country and strong army' as something far in the future. At the same time he was saying that the young Korean leaders should learn from Japan and aim to modernize their country. It was not surprising that he should have regarded China as an enemy but thought he could assist Korean modernization. The Japanese Foreign Ministry, especially diplomats posted to Korea, acted on the same basis.

Both now and in the past, however, the press tends to use exaggerated expressions. Fukuzawa, who developed his own arguments on the pages of a paper called *Jiji Shinpō* (News on Current Events), was the same. He did not say that Korea should be brought over to the Japanese side while China was weak, but he proclaimed that Japan had a duty to defend China and Korea against encroachment upon Asia by the great powers of Europe and America. In the previously cited pamphlet *Jiji Shōgen*, Fukuzawa argued broadly along the following lines:

> The fact that the Western countries, wielding great strength, are encroaching on the East is like a fire that is spreading. Even so, the Eastern countries, especially our neighbours China and Korea, are so stupid that they are not able to resist the Western powers, and this is like a wooden house that is unable to withstand a conflagration. Therefore, to help these countries with military force is not just

for their sakes, but is necessary also for Japan itself. We must defend them by force of arms, encourage them by means of education, and have them assimilate modern civilisation by learning from the Japanese example. If it should be unavoidable, we may have to threaten them by force.

Here Fukuzawa placed China and Korea in the same category, and argued that they should be protected and forced into civilization. In so doing he let his pen run away from him, and clearly toppled out of the ring. While he mistook the pace of Chinese modernization, he probably did not really believe that 'China' could be protected and reformed by the might of Japan. The whole of this piece seems to have been written with 'Korea' alone in his sight.

China becoming a 'strong power' – the Imo [Korean] or Jingo [Japanese] Incident

In fact it was the understanding of China by Yamagata Aritomo that was correct. In July 1882, a coup d'état by the anti-Japan faction in Korea took place, supported by the greater part of the population. The king, the Hŭngsŏn Taewôngun, expelled the pro-Japan faction from within the government, and in sympathy a crowd surrounded the Japanese legation and some people threw stones.

Guarding the legation was a duty of the Korean government, but the anti-Japanese authorities regarded the discharge of that duty negatively. The officials of the legation, cut off from outside sources of information, became panic-stricken, set their own legation on fire and in a group of twenty-eight fled and demanded protection at the Royal Palace. But since the gates of the Palace were closed, and there was no reply, they found their way to the port of Incheon, were taken on board a British survey vessel, and returned to Japan. While this was happening, several officials of the legation and four Japanese officers helping train Korean troops were killed. This is an outline of the Imo (Jingo) Incident, based on a report by Kondō Shinsuke, secretary of the Japanese legation.

Japan, which had aimed to defend Korea against encroachment by the great powers (in fact by China) and promote its development, was forced to abandon its legation temporarily and return to Japan, undoubtedly because of anti-Japanese sentiment increasing among the Korean government and people. For the Japanese government this was a rather humiliating episode.

On the other hand, the Japanese government at that time had no intention of going to war against the Chinese government, which was behind the incident. The Chinese government, moreover, took the Taewôngun away to China and returned the situation to what it had been before. As a result, because of Chinese interference, the Chemulp'o Treaty (the Remedial Treaty between Japan and Korea concerning the mutiny in Keijō [Seoul] in 1882) was signed, and the Korean government permitted the punishment of the perpetrators of the attack on the Japanese legation, as well as acknowledging the presence of Japanese troops within the legation to protect it and the payment of compensation to Japanese victims.

This, however, did not mean that things settled down.

First of all, the influence of China, which had played an important role in settling the affair, increased in relation to the government of Korea. China, on a continuous trajectory towards great power status, was able to send a large army to Korea, following a request from the Chinese Consul in Korea, Yuan Shih-Kai (formally a request from the Korean government).

Second, the Japanese legation, the domestic military and press, developed an increased antipathy to China. Already, as in the case of Fukuzawa, they could no longer speak tediously of defending 'China and Korea' from the great powers of Europe and America.

Towards naval rearmament

As I have already remarked, the Japanese Army and Navy from before the Imo (Jingo) Incident were concerned about the progress of China towards great power status. Naturally, following the incident, the navy demanded that it be allowed to expand, and specifically asked the government to import twenty-four warships over a three-year period. To this demand the navy minister, Kawamura Sumiyoshi, spoke about this expansion being aimed against Chinese expansion, as follows:

> If we look at the recent situation of China, it is striving to achieve power through military development, and is building up its navy at a much faster rate than in the past. The large and small warships that it is building today amount to more than 60 vessels, and in addition the warships, gunships, and torpedo vessels that it is currently constructing at home and abroad are beyond counting.[5]

This statement of opinion was written in November 1882, in the middle of the ultra-tight financial policies of the Finance Minister Matsukata Masayoshi (known as the Matsukata deflation). In the Ministry of Finance there was no scope to import twenty-four ships over three years, and only three ships per year, making nine over three years, were permitted.

The trend, however, was clearly in the direction of building up the navy in order to confront China.

Among the press, the man who was supporting and encouraging naval expansion to combat China was Fukuzawa Yukichi. He now casually abandoned the argument in his article published one year and two months earlier in *Jiji Shōgen*, in which he had argued that Japan should protect 'China and Korea' against the great powers of Europe and America. In November 1882 he published a pamphlet entitled *Heiron* (On the Military), in which he sounded the alarm about the progress of China towards great power status.

We know very well today that newspaper reporters, rather than philosophers, are quick to change their position. Fukuzawa, however, made what he had himself written just over a year earlier the target of criticism, and was a reporter who reduced researchers to tears. In this booklet Fukuzawa overturned what he himself had written in *Jiji Shōgen*, now writing in the following terms:

> The belittling idea that Chinese are weaklings is habitual among military men, but misses the mark entirely. Even among political scientists there are many who scorn Chinese people, but this cannot be taken seriously. These political scientists express themselves as follows:
>
> In order to strengthen the military and defend the people, unity of the national spirit is essential. The only way to unite the national spirit is for every one of the people to think about politics and promote the idea of national defence. Chinese political culture is quite the reverse of this.
>
> If we summarise this, under an autocratic government there can be no strong military, but this is merely an empty academic argument. If we are talking in hundreds of years, this may be correct, but their development of military forces is taking place urgently and realistically before our very eyes. The truth is surely that 'whether it is the military under a repressive government or the military under a liberal government, the strong prevails and the weak are defeated'.[6]

His conclusion amounts to a crude example of 'he who has the power has the right', but this is not the issue. In broad terms Fukuzawa had maintained that China, which he criticized for the backwardness of its civilization at the popular level, was unable to build up its military forces. This was his own argument a little over a year before, as I have shown. In *Heiron*, Fukuzawa turns this on its head, and argues that while at the popular level Chinese civilization is backward, even if it is ruled by a dictatorship, a strong country is strong and now China is a strong country.

We may readily surmise that the reason for this crucial change in Fukuzawa's position was China's power demonstrated in the Imo (Jingo) Incident, as well as the retreat of the pro-Japan faction in Korea. What is important is that Fukuzawa had borrowed from Yamagata, the chief of the general staff, his *Rinpō heibi ryaku* (Military Preparations and Strategy of Neighbouring Powers), and had written *Heiron*, which was based on it. In this book he made nearly 400 citations from *Rinpō heibi ryaku*.[7] Shortly after his book was published he wrote to Yamagata, thanking him for according him the ability to peruse such materials, and he promised to send him several copies of his own book.[8]

Breakdown in the reform of Korea – the Kapsin [Korean] or Kōshin [Japanese] Incident

Neither the Japanese military nor diplomats posted to Korea, nor indeed writers such as Fukuzawa, lowered the banner of 'reforming Korea', or of 'protection'. Their adversary, however, was no longer the great powers of Europe and America, but their powerful Asian enemy, China. 'Asianism', meaning confronting advances into Asia by the great powers of Europe and America, was difficult to legitimize.

Japan and China were confronting each other over control of Korea, where a pro-Japan faction and a pro-China faction were at loggerheads. This resembled a situation where China opened hostilities against France in Vietnam over the right to control Annam. In December 1884, the Japanese legation, forced into an inferior position within Korea following the Imo (Jingo) Incident, together with the Korean pro-Japan faction including Park Yŏnghyo and Kim Okkyu, pressed ahead with a coup d'état, taking advantage of a favourable situation. This was the Kapsin (Kōshin) Incident. Park Yŏnghyo occupied the Royal Palace, and asked the Japanese legation to send troops to protect the king. The force defending the Japanese legation, on its own initiative, protected the king who was in his detached palace. Appointed by the king who was being 'protected' by the Japanese legation, Park organized a new cabinet.

China, however, having become a 'strong power', together with the Korean pro-China faction now excluded from power, easily suppressed the coup. The Chinese minister, Yuan Shih-Kai – leading a force of about 600 men, about four times that of the Japanese defensive force – attacked the Royal Palace, and snatched the king from the hands of the Japanese forces. The defeated Japanese side headed by the Minister Takezoe Shinichirō, and including about 150 men from the defensive force, the whole staff of the legation, and their families amounting to about 320 individuals, left the legation together, and found refuge at the Japanese consulate in Incheon. This is the outline of the Kapsin (Kōshin) Incident.

In this affair, the pro-Japan reform faction was removed, and in the power relationship between Japan and China, it was China that prevailed over Japan. This upended the relations hitherto between Japan, China and Korea. The alarm sounded at the end of 1880 by the headquarters director of the High Command, Yamagata Aritomo, had now come to pass.

If war breaks out, is victory assured?

Within Japan itself, sections of the press and some within the government, regarding this situation as humiliating, insisted that China be engaged in battle. Among them Fukuzawa's *Jiji Shinpō*, which argued that the Korean pro-Japan faction should be given backing, was the most determined. An editorial immediately after the event (27 February 1884), titled 'If war breaks out, victory is assured', argued as follows:

> It is well known that the Chinese military system is corrupt. . . . Its total establishment is said to be a million men, but in fact the numbers equipped with Western-style weapons and trained in their use is no more than fifty or sixty thousand. When they say that they have over a hundred warships, that is four times the number in the Japanese Navy, but in fact their gunships are paper tigers and they are mere decorations in the Pacific. They may be made of steel, but the men who use them are like puppets.
>
> Against them in the Japanese armed forces there are 40,000 regular soldiers and together with reserves this makes a total of 150,000 officers and men. If these prove insufficient, then 400,000 brave and resolute men remain from the former samurai. If war comes with China, it will not be difficult to find 500,000 well trained troops consisting of both regular soldiers and soldiers from among the former samurai. . . . If we win such a war, the prestige of Japan will immediately resound in the East, and in distant parts of Europe and America we shall be respected. . . . As a civilised and prosperous partner of the West in so many ways, we are likely to be looked up to as the leaders of the East.[9]

As I noted earlier, just two years earlier Fukuzawa, relying on help from Yamagata Aritomo, came to understand the true strength of the Chinese Army and Navy

(*Heiron*). Once Japan was overwhelmed by China and forfeited control of Korea, he lost the objectivity that he had previously exhibited.

Of course, what is recorded in *Fukuzawa Yukichi zenshū* does not mean that what appeared in the editorials in *Jiji Shinpō* were all written by Fukuzawa himself. But it is sure that Fukuzawa agreed with the publication of these editorials. The writer of these editorials added the following note:

> My hope as just one person living in Japan today, is to deliver independence for this country. If this hope can be realised, I shall not only be delighted, but shall willingly die in Peking. My resources should be put without regret towards military expenditure. Everybody in Japan feels like this. This affair in Korea has broken out, and if there should be war between Japan and China, I can assert confidently that Japan will win.[10]

Once war between Japan and China came close, the press became more favourable to war than it had been before.

Avoidance of war by Itō Hirobumi – the Tianjin Treaty

There were quite a number of people even within the government who went along with the hard line being taken by the press. Just as in the time of the Taiwan expedition ten years before, the forces of the former Satsuma domain centred on the navy were of this opinion.

The government at that time preceded the establishment of a cabinet system, the court noble Sanjō Sanetomi was prime minister, and Prince Arisugawa no Miya Taruhito of the Imperial Household was Minister of the Left (the position of Minister of the Right was vacant following the death of Iwakura Tomomi). Below them politicians from the former Chōshū domain and the former Satsuma domain served as councillors of equal rank. Since there were no councillors except for those from the two former domains, it was entirely a Sat-Chō (Satsuma-Chōshū) government, but the councillors from the two factions were not 'ministers', their powers were equal, and their numbers similar. From the former Chōshū domain there were Itō Hirobumi, Inoue Kaoru, Yamagata Aritomo and Yamada Akiyoshi, and from the former Satsuma domain Saigō Tsugumichi, Kawamura Sumiyoshi, Ōyama Iwao and Matsukata Masayoshi. Since, apart from Matsukata, councillors from the former Satsuma domain, much like the press, supported going to war, the position of the Chōshū faction opposed to the war was fairly problematic.

Even so, for the Chōshū faction councillors including Itō, fighting a war against China was out of the question.

First of all, it would have no legitimacy. As I have previously mentioned, in the Kapsin (Kōshin) Incident, the defensive force protecting the Japanese legation in Korea, following a request from the Korean coup d'état regime, sent troops to protect the Korean king, who was outside their jurisdiction. Seen from the perspective of the Korean government that had been overthrown in the coup, the Japanese legation and its defensive force formed part of the coup d'état.

If the coup government had been overthrown by the military force of the former Korean regime, that would have been an entirely legitimate action, and the Japanese legation, its defensive force and the Japanese government would have been placed in a position where its responsibility could be pursued by the new regime.

Luckily, it was not powerful enough in Korea, and since it had to rely on the military strength of the Chinese legation, relations between Japan and China were on a fifty-fifty basis. Protection of the Korean king by the Japanese defensive force clearly exceeded its legitimate powers, but the attack on the Japanese troops, not by Korean forces but by Chinese forces, was also difficult to define as legitimate action.

The affair could not be resolved except by sharing the pain between Japan and China, but as I have noted earlier, unanimous readiness to criticize by the indignant press, which did not know all the facts, meant that politicians needed to emerge with the capacity to persuade councillors and military men from the Satsuma faction, who were engaged in a struggle for power within the government. It was the Councillor Itō Hirobumi of the Chōshū faction who undertook the role that had been played ten years earlier, in 1874, by Ōkubo Toshimichi. Itō as a plenipotentiary negotiator between Japan and China set sail from Yokohama in February 1885, and from 4 April negotiated in Tianjin with the Chinese plenipotentiary Lee Hung Chang.

Before he received plenipotentiary status, Itō was well aware of the development of public opinion and of the hard-line faction within the government. In a letter dated January 1885 to his good friend Inoue Kaoru, Itō wrote as follows:

> At this point I think it is necessary to pay attention to fluctuations in domestic public opinion. Inflammatory newspaper editorials assert that the upheaval in Korea is the fault of China and Korea, and especially that the fault lies mainly with China, and there are biased assertions almost every day that blow up the affair out of proportion. These have a considerable impact. People who

are ignorant of the facts of this affair and sow doubts about it exist in every prefecture, particularly among former samurai, and can also be found among military men and bureaucrats within the central government.

This letter was dated 21 January, but Itō left Yokohama on 28 February in a determined mood, and was directing his attention to negotiations with Lee Hung Chang.

The negotiations between Lee and Itō began on 4 April, involving major concessions on Itō's side, and ended on 18 April with the completion of the Tianjin Treaty. I will omit a detailed examination of the circumstances, and confine myself to stating its contents. It consisted of three articles: Article 1: Withdrawal of Japanese and Chinese forces from Korea; Article 2: Cessation of the despatch of officers and men of both States to train Korean forces. Article 3: In the case of a situation in which either State needed to send troops to Korea, that State would send official notification to the other. According to the Historical Dictionary of Japanese Foreign Policy, 'official notification' meant 'informing each other mutually'.[11]

The meaning of this treaty is clear. It was a treaty to stop military interference in Korea by Japan and China. By means of this treaty the tension that had arisen between Japan and China was indeed calmed for a while.

But a definition of 'send official notification to the other' involved at that time a presentiment of an all-out war. This is because it could be read as meaning, when troops were despatched, 'a declaration of war'. Until that happened, both sides in appearance were maintaining peace, but behind the scenes were inevitably expanding their military capacity.

4

The Sino-Japanese War

The birth of 'Empire' and the continuation of 'Constitution'

In Part 1, Chapters 1 and 3, I analysed the history of about eleven years of confrontation between Japan and China, from the Taiwan expedition in 1874 to the Tianjin Treaty of 1885, and in Chapter 2 the vicissitudes of the democratic movement between 1875 and 1881.

Tracing the mutual relations between 'Empire' and 'Constitution' is the aim of this book, but while they were mutually related, at the same time there were independent variables in each. In foreign policy there was a foreign policy logic and in domestic politics a domestic politics logic. I examined their separate aspects in Chapter 3, and where necessary followed the procedure of dealing with their mutual relations. But in Chapter 4, which relates to the end of Part I, I want to discuss the history of Empire and the history of democratization in the same chapter. This is in order to make the book's plan clearer, and moreover, compared with the period covered in Chapter 3, in the period covered in this chapter, relations between Empire and Constitution were closer.

Towards military expansion before launching the Diet

In pre-war Japan, a public pledge by the Emperor had absolute significance. In one aspect, this supports the position advocated by post-war Japanese research into modernization of 'Emperor absolutism'.

On the other hand, in October 1881 the Emperor promised that the Diet would be inaugurated nine years later in 1890, and that however much the international situation might change, in 1890 the Diet must open its doors. 'Emperor absolutism', in order to defend the Emperor's pledge, had to become 'Emperor constitutionalism'.

In order to launch the Diet, it was necessary to establish a constitution. According to the thinking of 'popularism', opposed to 'Emperor absolutism', the essential thing was first to hold a popular assembly, to debate a constitutional draft there, and decide on a constitution. Even at that time, however, counting only adult males in Japan, their number totalled more than ten million, and it would have been impossible to gather them all together. Some sort of representative system would have been essential. But in order to decide the basis of a representative system, they would have had to put a constitution in place first.

For details on this I refer to my book *Nihon kindai shi* (Modern Japanese History),[1] but if I may just give my conclusion, at the height of the Popular Rights Movement between 1880 and 1881, its fundamental way of thinking about Constitution and Diet was divided into three.

First of all, the proposal of the conservative faction, which was the government's mainstream, was that before the Diet was inaugurated, it should be established in the name of the Emperor that government authority should be strong and Diet authority should be weak. They spoke of an 'authorized constitution' established by the Emperor and proclaimed by him to the people. What should be remembered, however, is that even in such a conservative constitution, the power of debating the budget was granted to the Diet set up in 1890. In other words, from 1890, without the approval of the Diet, expansion of the army and navy could not occur.

Second, there was the centrist argument about the Constitution, which before the 1881 Political Change was presented by the liberal faction in the government, and after 1881 by the *Rikken Kaishintō* (henceforth *Kaishintō*) founded by the centrist faction including Ōkuma Shigenobu. This differed from that of the conservative faction, and was a draft constitution set clearly in the framework of a parliamentary cabinet system, but because its popular support was weak, it was not much of a threat to the conservatives including the army and navy.

The problem was the third element, namely the radical faction, which had little interest in the constitution as such. Rather than the constitution, this group aimed to gain control of the House of Representatives, and it was consolidating its support among agricultural landlords and local notabilities.

This group, of the *Jiyūtō* tendency, before and after conclusion of the Tianjin Treaty in 1885, affirmed as its central policy aim 'financial retrenchment' and 'mitigating people's burdens' (reducing administrative expenditure and cutting taxation). Calling for reductions in administrative spending and tax cuts (land tax), they gathered support from rural landlords.

The principal opponent of the conservative faction, which included the army and the navy, was this radical faction. It was expected from earlier on that this group would probably command a majority when the Diet was inaugurated in 1890. In that case, after 1890, however great the 'threat' from China might be for Japanese foreign policy, in a Diet that was demanding retrenchment of administrative expenses, a military budget aimed at increasing the size of the armed forces was unlikely to pass.

Two points make this clear.

The first point is that for the government side, it was necessary to build up the army and navy before the inauguration of the Diet in 1890 (more accurately, before the budget debate in the House of Representatives in 1891). At the time of the conclusion of the Tianjin Treaty in 1885, it was clear on the government side that in the Constitution that was to be established in 1889 there would be a clause allowing a government to carry on with the budget of the previous year if its budget were defeated. In circumstances where the budget could not be passed (for instance, because the government and the Diet proved unable to reach a compromise), this clause would enable the budget of the previous year to come into effect. Once the Diet had come into existence, the agreement of the Diet would be necessary for army and navy expenditures to be increased. Moreover, it would be almost impossible to obtain such an agreement, and so if expenditure were increased in advance, army and navy expenditures could be protected (up to the level of the previous year) through the working of the clause permitting the government to carry on with the budget of the previous year.

I do not know how clearly government officials recognized this, but over a full four years between 1886, the year after the Tianjin agreement with China, and the opening of the Diet in 1890, the Japanese government set about fulfilling its plan to import forty-eight warships from Europe and America. This involved the floating of public bonds on four occasions. Thus when the Diet was inaugurated in 1890, military expansion in preparation for war with China was essentially complete.

Dispute between the House of Representatives and the government – stagnation of military expansion

Second, for several years after the Diet was inaugurated in 1890, army and navy rearmament in preparation for war with China came to a halt (new budget expenditure was now difficult). This was because of the policies of financial retrenchment and reducing tax burdens on the part of the *Jiyūtō* and *Kaishintō*, which between them enjoyed a majority in the House of Representatives. This could be expected, but whether it would continue indefinitely could perhaps be de-linked from China.

In the Japanese Imperial Constitution (Meiji Constitution), for which Itō Hirobumi and the head of the Cabinet Secretariat, Inoue Kiyoshi, had borrowed the expertise of foreign advisers, the provision in article 71 allowing the government to carry on using the budget of the previous year, as well as the clause forbidding irresponsible use of the Diet, was drafted. For instance, the government could veto reductions in administrative expenditure (article 67). But as well as arguing for constitutional government, it did not deny the powers of the Diet on increasing the size of the budget and on land tax increases. If they did not accept it, everyone would lose interest in the Diet, so that establishing the Constitution and setting up the Diet would lose all meaning. Wherever one looks in the seventy-six articles of the Constitution of the Great Japanese Empire, there is no article permitting the government capriciously to increase expenditure on the army and navy.

In a process that drew derisive comment concerning a weak point in the Imperial Constitution, during debates on the 1891 budget, and similarly on the 1892 budget, the House of Representatives pressed the government to reduce administrative expenditure by 10 per cent, and when the government refused to concede this, the House blocked acceptance of expenditure especially for warships for the navy. Boxed into a corner by this, the government dissolved the House of Representatives at the end of 1891, and interfered in the elections, even using the power of the police force, but in the elections of 15 February of the following year, factions opposing the government scored a victory. In the third Diet (the brief special session following the dissolution), and in the fourth Diet (November 1892–February 1893), the House of Representatives demanded a reduction in administrative spending, and so long as the government would not accept this, the House continued refusing to accept increased spending on warships.

These head-on clashes between the government and the House of Representatives were reported to their own government by the Chinese legation in Tokyo. Moreover because of these clashes, Japanese expenditure on warships would not – in the legation's opinion – increase at all. It may be inferred that Chinese concern about Japan weakened as a result.

Of course, some efforts were made to eliminate such head-on clashes between the government and the House of Representatives. Between the second

Itō Hirobumi cabinet of the time and the executive of the leading party in the House, the *Jiyūtō*, negotiations for a compromise to put paid to this situation of deadlock were going on behind the scenes.

Even so, the positions of the government proclaiming 'Prosperous country and strong army' and those of the majority parties in the House of Representatives (*Jiyūtō* and *Kaishintō*) were diametrically opposed, so that it was a mammoth task to find a compromise.

At this time a great deal of insistence on foreign threats, and fanning of nationalism, was to be found in government circles. However, as I have already stressed, since the Japanese people in general underestimated Chinese power, China did not become a target for nationalism.

Of course, even in Japan before the Diet was inaugurated, there was some trumpeting of nationalism. But this nationalism took as its adversary the great powers of Europe and America, so that it consisted of opposing excessive import of Western culture, and calling for Japanese traditions to be respected. 'Prosperous country, strong army' – the slogan broadcast by the Meiji government – meant absorbing Western civilization which the others opposed, with a view to creating a modern State that would impress the Western powers. So it was hardly compatible with that sort of nationalism.

That nationalism, in policy terms, meant 'diligence, thrift and militarism', in other words cutting waste, 'mitigating the people's burdens' and inculcating in the people a desire to defend the nation. The majority parties in the House of Representatives opposed to the government, arguing for cutting administrative costs and 'mitigating the people's burdens', were closer to this. Nationalism was not helping the government in its preparations for war with China.

The Imperial Edict on Harmony and Cooperation

If this was the case, the lack of functionality in the Constitution that had been established in the name of the Emperor – a situation in which rearmament aimed at China was not progressing at all – could only be solved in the name of the Emperor. The 'Edict on harmony and cooperation' issued on 10 February 1893, unlike the two edicts already discussed, has not been noticed much by researchers into modern Japanese history, but for naval rearmament in preparation for war with China, it had a most important meaning.

There were three important points in this edict.

The first was its insistence on the importance of foreign relations. The following statement by the Emperor demonstrates this:

> When I look back, the progress of the world's great powers accelerates from day to day. At this time within Japan conflict continues, while if the main aims of this country are forgotten, and the opportunity to increase our national prosperity is misunderstood, then I must apologise before the tombs of my ancestors, since this is not the way to achieve a good constitutional result.[2]

Here the expression 'the progress of the world's great powers' is used, but this must be understood to mean 'the progress of China'. To understand the real intention of bombastic expressions is important even today.

The second point is that (although I will not go into detail on this here) the government's unwillingness to reduce existing government expenditure was correct from a strict interpretation of the Constitution, and the Emperor himself intended to pressure the government on his own initiative concerning 'various administrative rectifications', in the words he used. To the government he was providing his 'name', but to the House of Representatives he was promising 'substance'.

The third point – the most important for this book which focuses on the history of relations between Japan and China – is the following item in the Edict. It is a little hard to read, but I cite it in a form close to the original.

> Concerning national military defence, each day that passes leaves a hundred years of shame. Here I am reducing Palace expenses, paying three hundred thousand yen to the Government every year over six years, and I order civil and military servants, excepting those in special circumstances, to pay ten per cent of their salary over this same period of six years, in order to contribute to the construction of naval vessels.[3]

Therefore it was an edict wishing the Diet to accept the government's proposal for costs of building warships.

Europeanization and nationalism

During the fourth Diet, when this edict was issued, the *Jiyūtō*, the largest party, had 90 seats out of 300. The *Kokumin Kyōkai*, which supported the government, occupied seventy seats. As I have touched on before, the 'Edict on Harmony and Cooperation' was the product of behind-the-scenes compromise negotiations between the second Itō government and the *Jiyūtō*, after which the *Jiyūtō* and the

Kokumin Kyōkai together controlled 160 seats out of 300, and the government could probably concentrate on preparing for war with China.

Things, however, did not proceed as smoothly as expected. In order to go to war with China, it was insufficient just to overcome domestic political conflict. It was necessary for the great powers of Europe and America, including its core, Great Britain, to take a position of benevolent neutrality.

If Great Britain were to agree to revise the unequal treaty it signed with Japan at the end of the Bakumatsu period, this would be a sign that Great Britain was supporting Japan. The foreign minister of the time, Mutsu Munemitsu, at the end of the fifth Diet, made a speech in which he spoke as follows (29 December 1893):

> In order to attain the goal of treaty revision, we must have foreign countries recognise our country's progress, our country's enlightenment, evidence that Japan has a special place within Asia and that it is a civilised and strong power. This is the great goal of achieving treaty revision.[4]

To make the Western powers recognize that Japanese Europeanization and Americanization was superior to that of China was the significant point about treaty revision.

Against this kind of 'Europeanization' there was a strong nationalist reaction. These protestors argued that in revising the treaties Japan should at no time seek to curry favour with Europe and America, or allow Japanese tradition to be destroyed, but that the unequal treaties in their current form should be put into force to the letter, so that Europeans, Americans and others living in Yokohama, Kōbe and elsewhere should be confined to special residence areas, commerce and travel should be brought to an end, and on these conditions they would raise their voices in support of treaty revision.

The *Kokumin Kyōkai*, which had supported the policy of 'Prosperous country, strong Army' as the pro-government party, and at the same time as a fiercely Nationalist Party, agreed with the argument that 'the current treaties should be strictly enforced'. At the time of the aforementioned 'harmony and cooperation edict', the *Kokumin Kyōkai*, which with the ninety-seat *Jiyūtō*, was a party supporting the second Itō government, at the end of the fifth Diet in the same year, became a party opposed to the government. It had sixty-eight seats, or almost the same number as in the previous Diet. When we add the seats belonging to other parties out of power, including the *Kaishintō*, a majority of seats in the House of Representatives were controlled by the faction-supporting maintenance of the existing treaties.

Not only in the Diet, but also in the press, there was strong support for 'enforcing the treaties'. In May 1894, 176 representatives of 76 newspapers and magazines throughout the country issued a statement strongly supporting the 'treaty enforcement' faction.

Anti-European and anti-American nationalism itself was not a direct impediment to the government's policy of 'prosperous country, strong army', nor to preparations for war with China. But as Prime Minister Itō and Foreign Minister Mutsu expected, it was clearly an impediment to the receipt of international praise for Japanese modernization. It was only the government that was calling for Europeanization, while Japanese public opinion was opposed to it, and this was because it was opposed to treaty revision.

It was impossible to keep the press quiet, but the government, without compromising with the House of Representatives, piled dissolution upon dissolution. In December 1893, it dissolved the fifth Diet, and in June 1894, after a general election, it dissolved the sixth Diet. Over the three and a half years from the opening of the Diet, the House of Representatives was dissolved three times.

Towards the Sino-Japanese War

The Chinese government, which had received reports from its legation in Japan about the divided conditions within Japan, in June 1894, some nine years after the Tianjin Treaty, received a request from the Korean government to suppress the peasant revolt known as the Tonghak Party uprising. It sent troops to Korea and reported this to the Japanese government as required by the Tianjin Treaty. It seems that they judged that the Japanese government would not be able to react by sending troops.

There was a certain logic in this calculation by the Chinese government. The dispute between the government and the House of Representatives from the end of 1893 to May 1894, unlike on previous occasions, was a conflict about whether to adopt a conciliatory approach to the Western powers, or a hard-line attitude. The government took the former option, whereas six parties excluding the *Jiyūtō* (at the time known as the 'six hard line factions') supported the latter.

If it had been nationalism opposed to the great powers of Europe and America, I think it would have made sense for Japan to adopt a friendly attitude towards China, its neighbour in East Asia. But when we already examined the circumstances leading to the Tianjin Treaty, we saw that the Japanese press regarded China as an enemy and despised it. The 'Treaty enforcement faction', immediately before the Sino-Japanese War (the first Japan–China War), was the same. It criticized the Itō government for its failure to control Korea in the Imo (Jingo) and Kapsin (Kōshin) episodes, and in the Tianjin Treaty for having been made by China to swallow a humiliating treaty, but they seemed to be in no hurry to revise the treaties with the powerful states of Europe and America.

A speech to the sixth Diet by Inukai Tsuyoshi, revered as the so-called God of the Constitution, in words that are too embarrassing to quote, spoke of the inferiority of China. Their nationalism was directed against the great powers of Europe and America, but it was a nationalism that entirely lacked any feeling of joining together with Korea and China to defend Asia against Europe and America.

This kind of nationalism that opposed Europeanization and Americanization changed direction once war broke out with China and took on the character of total support for the war and an end to criticism of the government.

The Chinese government notified Japan on 6 June 1894 of its despatch of troops, and the Japanese government notified China of its despatch of troops to protect its legation on the 7th, but before both governments had issued notifications, they had both already sent troops to Korea. Chinese troops, however, continued to arrive by land ahead of troops from Japan, and when Japanese forces reached the Korean capital Keijō (now Seoul), the Tonghak Party uprising had already been suppressed by forces from China.

Nevertheless, the Japanese government strengthened its determination to engage in total war with China.

As I have already made clear, ever since the Japanese government had been buffeted by press criticism, had signed the Tianjin Treaty and been constrained to withdraw its troops from Korea, it embarked on rearmament, with China in its sights as a potential enemy. In the 'Harmony and Cooperation Edict' of February 1893, discussed earlier in this chapter, demanding that the House of Representatives support construction of warships (for which the Emperor had gone so far as to cut his Palace expenses), this was not meant for war in which Great Britain would be the adversary. The Japanese government, over the whole of nine years from the Tianjin Treaty, had been preparing for war with China.

In a letter dated 27 June from Foreign Minister Mutsu to Prime Minister Itō, the determination of the government to make war is evident:

> The Chinese troops despatched to Korea may be seen as an indication of self-confidence, but the central Government seems to be avoiding despatch

of additional troops. In spite of assuming that an explosion between Japan and China cannot be avoided in the near future, we ought not to miss this opportunity. From ancient times there is no shortage of examples where to enhance its reputation a nation gives a chance to its enemy. . . . Since this is a clash that we absolutely cannot avoid, this confrontation should take place now, at a time favourable to our country.[5]

Opposition from the Meiji Emperor

In this way the government decided to make war on China, and only one person opposed this. This was none other than the Meiji Emperor. I have already discussed how, a year and a half before, he had persuaded the House of Representatives not to oppose naval rearmament, using the power of an Imperial Edict, but the Meiji Emperor should not be remembered for this case alone. Even though it did not affect the subsequent cabinet decision, he showed strong reluctance to countenance war with China.

The government, at a cabinet meeting on 15 June, decided on two points: the first that it would not withdraw its troops until the Chinese side agreed to domestic reform of the Korean government promoted by both States together; second, if China did not agree to this, Japan would press ahead with such reform on its own initiative. Under the pre-war Constitution, a cabinet resolution on an important foreign policy issue lacked validity until there was a petition to the Throne and it had been given consent (article 13). On the same day Prime Minister Itō petitioned the Throne. The Emperor, however, did not immediately give his consent, but sending his Head Chamberlain, Tokudaiji Sanetsune, to Foreign Minister Mutsu, queried some doubtful points. According to a letter sent on the same day by Mutsu to Itō, the Emperor's doubts were the following:

> Just now, the Head Chamberlain Tokudaiji has come as messenger from the Emperor, and has raised certain questions about the petition. His Majesty the Emperor has a particular concern about the future situation. In particular, the Emperor is concerned about the last section of the petition, positing the refusal to withdraw our troops from Korea until negotiations between Japan and China have been concluded, as well as the point that the Japanese Government will unilaterally impose reform on the Korean Government if China does not agree to reform of the Korean Government by Japan and China together, . . . If it should happen that that the opinions of the Emperor and the Cabinet resolution are incompatible with each other, this would be a very disturbing situation. I

would appreciate it if Prince Itō would be so good as to visit the Emperor in the Palace tomorrow and persuade him face to face.[6]

On 16 June, Prime Minister Itō and Foreign Minister Mutsu successively visited the Palace, and persuaded the Emperor, so that he was able to give his consent to the cabinet resolution of the previous day.

This matter is important for two reasons.

First, the Meiji Emperor was neither an absolute ruler nor was he simply a robot. He did not have the power to overturn a resolution of the cabinet, but he did have sufficient power to express doubts and postpone his consent for about a day. This is an important point in understanding the Emperor system.

Second, the Meiji Emperor seems not to have accepted the kind of contemptuous view of China expressed by Inukai Tsuyoshi of the *Kaishintō*, mentioned earlier. This can be seen from his delay in giving consent to the cabinet resolution of 15 June. I also want to draw attention to another example, namely the actions that followed immediately after declaration of war against China on 1 August. The Emperor showed his opposition to the despatch of a messenger to announce the declaration of war at the Ise Shrine and at the grave of the late Emperor Kōmei. This is not well known and is rather difficult to understand, so I will quote a relevant section from the *Meiji tennō ki* (*Life of the Meiji Emperor*), the most reliable source on the actions of the Emperor (I have revised the text to make it easier to read):

> 11 August (Despatch of a messenger to the Ise Shrine and the grave of the Emperor Kōmei). After a declaration of war was made, when Hijikata Hisamoto, the Imperial Household Minister, paying his respects to the Emperor, asked His Majesty for a suitable person to report it at the Ise Shrine and the grave of the Emperor Kōmei, the Emperor replied: 'It is not necessary, we find this war disappointing. Since Ministers have declared that war is inevitable, we give our consent. Reporting this to the Shrine and at the grave of our ancestor is for us an exceedingly bitter thing.'[7]

When Hijikata remonstrated with the Emperor, asking whether it was not a mistake, after he had issued his edict declaring war, but causing a delay, the Emperor became angry and burst out: 'Do not mention this again! I do not wish to see your face again.'

Much like his opposition to the cabinet resolution of 15 June, the next day the Emperor changed his mind, ordered Hijikata to choose a messenger to be sent to the Palace and the grave, and when Hijikata went to the Palace, the Emperor greeted him 'With a bright countenance and not much changed from normal'.

In both cases the Meiji Emperor had postponed his decision by a day, but he expressed his disapproval of the war against China in a fairly trenchant fashion. His predecessor, the Emperor Kōmei, shortly before his death spoke of 'expelling the Western barbarians'. It was not right to report to the grave of this man that 'expulsion of the barbarian' was a policy being directed against China. The Meiji Emperor must have felt this strongly.

Despite such speculations, the Emperor on 1 August 1894 issued an edict declaring war against China, and sent a messenger to the Ise Shrine and the grave of the Emperor Kōmei. The Sino-Japanese War began.

The conclusion of the war

I will describe briefly the outcome of the war. The Japanese Army on 15 September 1894, in a general attack, forced Pyongyang to surrender, and swept the Chinese forces out of the Korean peninsula, and on 17 November the Japanese Navy, in a fierce engagement, put to flight the Chinese Beiyang Fleet, which was protecting the battleships Chih Yuen and Ching Yuen. The army, enthused by this naval victory, continued its advance towards the Liaodong Peninsula, and at the end of 1894 had occupied most of the same peninsula including the towns of Lushun (Ryōjun, Port Arthur) and Dalian (Dairen). At this point the trend of the situation had become quite clear. Around this time, as peace negotiations followed the Japanese victory, agitation began in Japan, not only for Korean 'independence' but also to defend the Chinese territory of the Liaodong Peninsula, which was to be ceded to Japan.

In February 1895, with the defeat of the Chinese Beiyang Fleet at Weihaiwei, the Sino-Japanese War had effectively reached its conclusion. In March of the same year, the Chinese plenipotentiary Li Hongzhang landed in Shimonoseki, and a peace conference began. The Japanese plenipotentiaries were Prime Minister Itō Hirobumi and Foreign Minister Mutsu Munemitsu. The plenipotentiaries of both nations entered into negotiations for a peace treaty. The positions of the plenipotentiaries of both sides regarding peace negotiations were diametrically opposed. Li Hongzhang, countering the demands of the Japanese side regarding conditions for peace, going over the heads of the Japanese plenipotentiaries, apparently appealed to various countries of Europe and America, and thus put forward demands following from contradictions.

(1) China recognizes the independence of Korea, but Japan must equally recognize the independence of Korea.

(2) Since Japanese war aims were confined to the independence of Korea, to partition Chinese territory is contradictory.
(3) The amount of reparations must be limited to 105,000,000 yen, which was the sum actually expended by Japan for this war.
(4) The demand for the cession to Japan of Taiwan, which Japan did not occupy during this war, is at variance with the demand for the Liaodong Peninsula, since Japan had already occupied it.
(5) Most favoured nation treatment in the commercial treaty must apply to both sides.

Against this the Japanese side insisted on its attitude that this was entirely a treaty between the victor nation and the vanquished nation, and there was no reason to reject the logic of the Japanese demands. The Japanese side on 10 April put their final offer on the table; on 17 April, Li Hongzhang also signed the final proposal. This was the Japan–China Peace Treaty (the Shimonoseki Treaty).

The Japan–China Treaty and the triple intervention

The principal contents of the Treaty were:

1. A guarantee of the independence of Korea.
2. Cession to Japan of the Liaodong Peninsula, Taiwan and Penghu (Hōkotō, Pescadores).
3. Payment of compensation of 200,000,000 taels (about 300,000,000 yen).
4. Shashih, Chungking, Soochow and Hangchow to be newly open, including opening their ports, accepting that commerce and industry, as well as freedom of residence, should apply to Japan, etc.

This final demand to open cities and ports was designed to gain British support.

Since in commercial treaties of various states of Europe and America, the most favoured nation treatment was included, the opening of cities and ports obtained by Japan in its commercial treaty with China would also be applied to the states of Europe and America. Therefore, Great Britain, which had the most abundant trade with China, decided in a cabinet resolution to reject a proposal from the Russian government to intervene jointly.

Russia, which enquired about an opportunity to intervene in southern Manchuria, was anxious about the Japanese intervention, and together with Germany and France warned Japan to withdraw from the Liaodong Peninsula (the Triple Intervention). The British government also refrained from supporting Japan against the triple intervention. It was out of the question to damage cooperative relations with Russia and France by involvement in an East Asian issue.

If Japan could not obtain British support, it was impossible to reject the three-nation representation, while to open hostilities with Russia, which had the world's largest army, was even opposed by the Japanese military. It was clear that the Diet and the press would criticize this acceptance of humiliating intervention, but there was no room to heed domestic opinion.

The Japanese government notified the three states that Japan would return the Liaodong Peninsula, and with this as the premise, on 8 May documents ratifying a Japan–China Peace Treaty were exchanged with the Chinese government.

Part II

The division between 'Empire' and 'Constitution'

Chronological table

Date	Events
1895	Shimonoseki Peace Conference; Shimonoseki Treaty signed; Triple intervention by Russia, Germany and France; conquest of Taiwan.
1896	Rikken Kaishintō, Rikken Kakushintō and others form Shinpotō (Ōkuma Shigenobu); first tax increase since Sino-Japanese War.
1898	Jiyūtō and Shinpotō in concert defeat tax increase proposal; Jiyūtō and Shinpotō merge to form Kenseitō; first Ōkuma (Ōkuma-Itagaki) Cabinet formed (first party cabinet); Kenseitō (former Jiyūtō) splits with Kenseihontō (former Shinpotō). Revision of land tax regulation (3.3 per cent increase); Germany leases Shandong Peninsula, Russia leases Liaotung Peninsula, Britain leases Wehaiwei.
1900	Electoral law revision (more than 10 yen tax payers given vote); military ministers to be serving officers; north China Incident (expedition against Boxer Rebellion); Rikken Seiyūkai formed (President Itō Hirobumi).
1902	First Anglo-Japanese Alliance treaty signed.
1903	Saionji Kinmochi becomes *Seiyūkai* president.
1904	Russo-Japanese War (to 1905); first Japan–Korea Agreement.
1905	Second Anglo-Japanese Alliance; Portsmouth Treaty (Russo-Japanese Peace Treaty); Hibiya Arson Incident; Second Japan–Korea Agreement.
1906	Southern Manchuria Railway Co. Ltd. (Mantetsu) founded.
1907	Post-war Depression; Imperial Defence Policy; Third Japan–Korea Agreement; First Japan–Russia Agreement.
1909	Itō Hirobumi assassinated in Harbin.
1910	Rikken Kokumintō founded (Inukai Tsuyoshi); Great Treason Incident; Korean Annexation Treaty; Korean government-general established; Terauchi Masatake first governor-general.
1911	Restoration of customs autonomy; Third Anglo-Japanese Alliance Treaty; Chinese Revolution.

(*Continued*)

Date	Events
1912	Death of Meiji Emperor; Chinese Republic established; Because proposal for two new army divisions rejected, Army Minister Uehara Yūsaku resigned; Saionji Cabinet dissolved, Katsura Cabinet formed; Taishō Political Change (first Constitutional Defence Movement).
1913	Katsura Tarō formed Rikken Dōshikai; Crowd surrounded Diet building, set alight police boxes and pro-government newspaper company offices.
1914	Siemens corruption Incident; House of Peers rejected budgetary proposal for naval rearmament.
1915	Twenty-one demands to China issued;
1916	'Great war boom' began; Kenseikai formed (Katō Takaaki).
1917	Ishii-Lansing Agreement; Russian Revolution.

Introduction

The system of apportionment between peace and democracy

Before covering in detail the conflicts between 'Empire' and 'Constitution' following the Sino-Japanese War, I want to present a brief outline of Part II as a whole.

The lifelong theme of Matsuo Takayoshi,[1] the leading researcher of Taishō Democracy (who passed away in December 2014), was 'constitutionalism at home by overcoming 'Empire abroad'. In other words, the objective of his research into Taishō Democracy was to place democrats opposed to imperialism in the centre of history and transmit this to his contemporaries.

Even so, the use by the press from the final year of Meiji into the first year of Taishō (1912–13), of the slogan 'Constitution at home, Empire abroad', was to affirm in tandem the annexation of Korea and expansion of Japanese interests in Manchuria and Mongolia (special interests that Japan had obtained following the Russo-Japanese War in Manchuria and Inner Mongolia) together with the simultaneous progress of democratization.

Of course Matsuno, having a good understanding of all this, presented Yoshino Sakuzō and his *Minponshugi* (politics *based* on the people),[2] which demanded of democrats that they oppose turning Korea into a colony and converting the Chinese territory of Manchuria into a semi-colony.

About twenty years ago (1995), in a lecture given by Matsuo at the Yoshino Sakuzō Hall, he spoke as follows:

> Among the four basic ideas of Yoshino Sakuzō, the third was the most problematic. Many people, including his supporters, had the same idea as his concerning the other three basic ideas, namely his advocacy of *minponshugi*, his support for the proletarian movement, and publication of the corpus of Meiji culture. But in his criticism of Japanese aggression against Korea and China, Yoshino, to put it strongly, was isolated and unsupported. . . . On this he was ignored, or regarded with hostility. For this reason alone, his third argument has an important contemporary significance. . . . I feel that the thinking of Japanese

people concerning East Asian peoples does not greatly differ between Yoshino's time and our own. If it is good just for Japan, people think it doesn't matter about other peoples, such as those of China and Korea. This bad tradition, particular to the Japanese, remains essentially unchanged.

What Matsuo was emphasizing here was the exceptional quality of Yoshino as the proponent of *Minponshugi*, in defining Taishō Democracy as 'Empire externally' by means of 'Constitution domestically'. But if we turn this upside down, we find that the whole of the domestic democratic movement known as 'Taishō Democracy' accepted 'Empire externally'. That which shows symbolically the symbiosis of 'Constitution domestically' but 'Empire externally' was that the opposition *Kenseikai* Party, which within the Diet supported the movement outside the Diet pressing for universal suffrage, continuously supported the twenty-one demands (made to China in 1915), ignoring the mainstream of international opinion. (At that stage it was the *Rikken Dōshikai*, but became the *Kenseikai*, in 1916, and supported it together with the *Chūseikai*, the *Kōyū Club* and others, until it made a comeback nine years later in 1924.) It can be said that the position of the *Rikken Seiyūkai* (henceforth *Seiyūkai*), which consistently opposed universal male suffrage, and aimed to have agreement not only with America but also with China, should be called 'non-Constitution domestically and non-Empire externally', whereas the position of the opposition *Kenseikai* was that of 'Constitution domestically, Empire externally'.

If we compare the *Seiyūkai* and the *Kenseikai* in terms of their domestic policies, it was the *Kenseikai* that was plainly the more democratic. But if we compare them in terms of the foreign policies, then the *Kenseikai* was the more imperialist. To express this subtle contradiction, we may say that Matsuo's 'Constitution in domestic policy, Empire in foreign policy' is inadequate as a framework for analysis.

*

It goes without saying that a generally accepted idea among us is that 'peace and democracy' should be seen as a single package. However, with the first constitutional defence movement in 1912 and 1913, once systemic rotation in office between the domain-faction bureaucrats and the *Taiseitō-Seiyūkai* had collapsed, the 'sharing of peace and democracy' between the *Seiyūkai* and the *Kenseikai*, in its own fashion and with mutual reinforcement, was raising the quality of politics.

The system under which the domain-faction bureaucrats (plus the military and the House of Councillors), together with the *Seiyūkai*, formed a cooperative regime between the two great forces of conservatism was called the 'Saionji-Katsura regime' (from the two leaders who more or less alternated in office). Under this system during the nine years (1905–14) from the end of the Russo-Japanese War to the outbreak of the First World War, popular rioting broke out on three separate occasions. It may perhaps be appropriate to call these riots a popular movement. They were not, however (and this includes the anti-Security Treaty struggle of 1960), peaceful in the manner of the 2015 demonstrations against the Security Treaty regime. As a result of the Sino-Japanese and Russo-Japanese Wars, 'Empire in foreign policy' made real progress, while 'Constitution in domestic policy' was merely used for its method of fulfilling a popular movement outside the Diet.

Later on, as I shall show in Part III, the 'sharing of peace and democracy' was overcome by the second constitutional defence movement. The *Kenseikai* ditched the concept of 'Empire externally', revising its foreign policies to encompass cooperation with Great Britain and the United States, and towards non-interference in the internal affairs of China. This was the emergence of the 'Shidehara diplomacy' (after Foreign Minister Shidehara Kijūrō). During the cabinet of three pro-Constitution parties led by Katō Takaaki, president of the *Kenseikai*, who successfully brought in the Universal Male Suffrage Law of 1925, the doctrine of 'Constitution domestically' made great strides. This was the first time in the pre-war period that 'peace' and 'democracy' were advocated by one and the same political party. Because of the defection in August of the same year of the *Seiyūkai* and the *Kakushin Club* from the cabinet of the three pro-Constitution factions, the *Kenseikai* formed a single-party cabinet. Most of the Democrat Yoshino Sakuzō's expectations came to be fulfilled in actual politics.

In pre-war Japan, however, the way forward for party cabinets (the 1925–7 *Kenseikai* Cabinet and the 1929–31 *Rikken Minseitō* Cabinet), based on the combination of 'peace and democracy', which should be seen as their key policies, was by no means clear. The opposition *Seiyūkai*, in the form of opposing the change of direction on the part of the *Kenseikai*, ceased to advocate a policy of 'non-Empire in foreign policy'. The *Seiyūkai*, ever since it had acquired as its president the Army General Tanaka Giichi in April 1925, transformed itself into a fully conservative party advocating 'Empire in foreign policy, Emperor-centred politics domestically'.

Not only had the *Seiyūkai* become more conservative, but also the *Kenseikai* line was being subjected to attack from the military. The navy, which had accepted disarmament under the Washington Treaty at the time of the Hara Kei and Takahashi Korekiyo cabinets of 1921–2, strongly contested the London Disarmament Treaty of 1930.

Nevertheless, the most important issue for this book, which is covering a swathe of modern Japanese history focusing on 'Empire and Constitution', was the demand of the military to expand its interests in Manchuria and Mongolia. I would like to make a distinction between having a special interest in Manchuria and actually possessing it. It is true that in its victory in the Sino-Japanese War in 1895, Japan's goal of 'Empire' expanded beyond Korea to Manchuria and Mongolia, but this was limited to the *maintenance* of its special interests in southern Manchuria and the eastern part of Inner Mongolia. With the formation of a cabinet of conservative parties in 1927 as its opportunity, the army demand changed to '*possession* of Manchuria and Mongolia'. The goal of 'Empire externally' had suddenly expanded. The division between 'Empire' and 'Constitution' in the title of Part II extended until just before the final collapse.

5

Strong army and war weariness
'Empire' and 'Constitution' before the Russo-Japanese War

'Constitution' did not aspire to 'Empire'

In the nine years from the end of the Sino-Japanese War until the Russo-Japanese War of 1904, the Japanese people may be seen as having to 'eat bitter fruit' (*gashin shōtan*) for the sake of taking revenge on the three states including Russia that had forced Japan to return to China the Liaotung Peninsula, which had been for Japan one of the spoils of war. It is well known that this four-character phrase, meaning endurance of hardships for the sake of a future reversal of fortune, was an expression widely used as a slogan at that time. During the same period, within a few years from the triple intervention, Russia established special rights in the Liaotung Peninsula and Germany established special rights in the Shandong Peninsula, so that intervention by the great powers was developing further.

The House of Representatives, however, in which the *Jiyūtō* and the *Shinpotō* (the party formed from a merger of the *Rikken Kaishintō* and other small groups) held a majority, continued to oppose increases in the land tax earmarked for army and navy rearmament over the three years following the Sino-Japanese War (1895–8). Even when, at the end of 1898, a section of the House of Representatives (the *Kenseitō*) changed its position to support such a spending boost, they imposed upon it a limit of five years. The year 1904 – five years from 1899 when the land tax was increased – was the year in which the Russo-Japanese War broke out. The faces of people swearing revenge against Russia and 'eating bitter fruit' were nowhere to be found.

In 1900, when the former *Jiyūtō*, which for many years had been central to the Popular Rights Movement, founded the *Rikken Seiyūkai* presided over by the elder statesman of the Restoration Itō Hirobumi, a transition seems to have been brought about from 'mitigating people's burdens' (reducing taxation) to 'strong Army, prosperous country'. But before the seventeenth Diet at the end of 1902, in which the end was approaching for the five-year time limit for increases in the land tax, the *Seiyūkai* expressed its opposition to an extension of the tax for the purposes of naval rearmament. In the Party's Congress on 4 December, its president, Itō, expressed the view that 'Naval rearmament should not depend on the land tax, but should be pursued by reducing other expenditure'.[1]

December 1902 was just a year and two months before the outbreak of the Russo-Japanese War, and was a full four years after the decision in December 1898 to increase land tax over a five-year period. Rather than naval rearmament in order to make war against Russia, which appeared to be coming closer, the *Seiyūkai* of Itō and Hara gave priority to defending the time limit on tax increases from four years before.

In the present writer's first book, titled *Meiji kenpō taisei no kakuritsu* (*The Establishment of the Meiji Constitutional System*, published in 1971),[2] I argued that the 'popular parties', namely the *Jiyūtō* and the *Shinpotō*, with the coming of the Sino-Japanese War, withdrew their demand to abolish land tax, fiercely resisting, however, efforts to increase land tax, but that the *Kenseitō* (the former *Jiyūtō*, later the *Seiyūkai*, led by Hoshi Tōru), in the end supported land tax increases, and while it was aiming to become the permanent party of the government, the 'Meiji constitutional system' was established. Even now I believe that my analysis was correct.

Nevertheless, from the standpoint of the present book, in which I develop a general view of Japanese modern history focusing on a confrontational axis between 'Empire' and 'Constitution', a rather different historical picture emerges. The policy changes from the *Jiyūtō* to the *Kenseitō* to the *Seiyūkai* was a story confined to domestic financial and economic policies, and was separate from the line of 'Empire' in foreign policy, meaning expansion into Korea and China, as well as fighting a war with Russia.

Hara Kei of the *Seiyūkai*, in a diary entry five days before the outbreak of the Russo-Japanese War (which began on 10 February 1904), wrote:

> If it comes to war, the people as a body should keep silent, and in today's situation the people must unite without demur, yet in present circumstances the majority of the people desire peace but they refrain from saying so. The same is true for the Elder Statesmen (*genrō*), except for a small minority, personally opposed to war, but in fact war is coming close day by day.[3]

This demonstrates the point in an extreme form.

Neither the government nor the people wanted to fight a war with Russia

Between 2015 and 2016 the Japanese people, perhaps for the first time in the seventy years since the end of the war, became conscious of 'war' as an issue. It probably did not seem obvious to anybody with which country the parliamentary 'war bill', which they themselves opposed, really might lead this country into war. But for the first time in seventy years, the idea that Japan might become involved in some kind of a war became a real matter for concern. I think that this concern will be groundless (but recently, it has become hard to know whether any of a number of major countries might light the touch-paper of war). However, even the present writer who is inclined towards optimism was amazed at this assertion of Hara Kei just before the Russo-Japanese War, when it would probably have been well known to contemporary Japanese that a majority of the Japanese people were demanding peace.

Moreover, Hara Kei's diary records that these were not just ordinary people. He said that the Elder Statesman Itō Hirobumi, Inoue Kaoru, and even anti-Russian hard-line polemicists in the first cabinet of Katsura Tarō thought that a war between Japan and Russia would not take place.

Since this so much resembles the contemporary situation, I want to quote the very words of Hara Kei himself. This is his diary for the day after Japan's declaration of war against Russia (11 February).

> Itō and Inoue have come to oppose the war, though they do not express this clearly. Ordinary people, however, particularly businessmen, hate the war, though they are not brave enough to say this openly. In this way the people's feelings are becoming inured to war. Some people in the Government are promoting the war for their own reputation. Although the majority of them dislike war in their hearts, they become unable to oppose what they have openly argued for.[4]

As we can see from this, the people did not demand the Russo-Japanese War, but they did not raise their voices protesting against it. Moreover within the government, there were few arguing for the war who really intended to go to war. But putting on a bold front about it meant that it was difficult to withdraw. If this was the case then who was it that was in command of the government and the people? It could be seen as the army, which for nine years, ever since the Sino-Japanese War, had been aiming to expand 'Empire', or as the navy, or as the government leadership in both countries, which overestimated the possibility of concessions on the part of the other.

Expansion of the army and navy following the Sino-Japanese War

Despite the feelings of war weariness among the Japanese people that I discussed in the previous section, in 1904–5 the Japanese Army and Navy had been rearming just to the extent that would make victory possible in a war against Russia. Widely used figures of casualties in the Russo-Japanese War of 118,000 killed in battle or who died later from wounds, and 91 vessels lost, also demonstrate just how far the army and navy, which had suffered that number of casualties, had been making preparations over those nine years. Over those same nine years, why was it that the House of Representatives, which had opposed increasing the land tax, and after the increases took place had continued to demand tax reductions, failed to oppose such an expansion of the army and the navy until the end of 1902?

Special circumstances existed at the time, similar to those of army and navy rearmament before the Diet was inaugurated, as described in Part I, Chapter 4. The House of Representatives went along with rearmament plans for the army and navy over the long period termed 'post-Sino-Japanese War Management' during the ninth Diet (December 1895–March 1896), which was held soon after the victory over China. The army plan, over the eight years from 1896 to 1903, was for 90,000,000 yen, while the naval plan was for 180,000,000 yen for the ten years between 1896 and 1905. The size of army and navy rearmament taken together of 270,000,000 yen, when compared with the 85,000 000 yen spent before the Sino-Japanese War, can easily be imagined. This plan for military rearmament was about three times larger.

Apart from the fact, however, that there was an eight-year plan and a ten-year plan, the 270,000,000 yen was allocated during each year of the plan as contingency expenditure within the total annual budget. It was not the case that 270,000,000 yen was spent in one lump sum as payment for army and navy rearmament. But the Diet, which had recognized the eight-year plan and the ten-year plan, did not have the power to debate this budget annually. The expenditure on rearmament for the army and the navy following the Sino-Japanese War was in a different category at that time.

Nevertheless, during the first Diet following the Sino-Japanese War, the *Jiyūtō* had its own particular reason for accepting in broad outline this long-term rearmament plan. Their source of funding did not depend on tax rises, but was a plan for compensation from China to demand 345,000,000 taels (about 40,000,000 yen), including 30,000,000 that had been paid as compensation from China for having returned to China the territorial cession of the Liaotung Peninsula.

Since the 'strong army' part of the 'strong Army, prosperous country' slogan meant paying through Chinese compensation and not imposing tax burdens on the people, this was hardly a strange argument in the House of Representatives, which mainly represented the interests of agricultural landlords. Moreover, agricultural landlords following the Sino-Japanese War had become comfortably wealthy because of increases in the price of rice, and had little patience with doctrines of extreme parsimony. However, the fact that they had fiercely opposed increases to land tax, as well as the fact that for them their acceptance of 'strong army' ambitions did not signify their support for war, is something that I have already discussed.

The ten-year plan for naval rearmament that began in 1896 was still valid at the end of 1902. So why was it that despite this a new naval rearmament plan emerged, as I have mentioned earlier?

Why did the navy speed up its rearmament?

Even just before the Sino-Japanese War, the government, thinking that naval rearmament concluded before the promulgation of the Diet was insufficient, and in conformity with the Emperor's Edict, obtained the agreement of the Diet. The fact that a similar situation should have arisen when the Russo-Japanese War became imminent is not difficult to imagine. The Japanese Navy, which had destroyed the Chinese fleet, was now demanding military force sufficient to destroy the Russian fleet.

The 'Empire' now in the course of construction, however, was pointed towards Korea and Manchuria, and the principal player in bringing it about was not the navy but the army. The fame of the *Kantōgun* (Kwantung Army – one of the colonial standing armies, a military detachment deployed in Manchuria, northeast China) was a symbol of this. Why was the Japanese Navy, which lacked the motivation to take Korea and Manchuria rapidly, in so much of a hurry to rearm?

Nakazato Hiroshi, who focused on the financial and defence policies of the first Katsura cabinet (1901–5),[5] which has been relatively thinly researched, insists on the importance of the secret agreement attached to the Anglo-Japanese Alliance, which did not make any assumption about the imminence of war between Japan and Russia. Following the conclusion of the Anglo-Japanese Alliance in January

1902, the foreign ministers of the two states exchanged secret communications, and they attached importance to the fact that they promised that 'in the seas of the Far East, they would maintain navies that would become superior to the navy of any third pose, in order to be able to combine together'.[6]

At the same time Nakazato points out that in 1902, when this secret agreement was signed, the navy had front loaded and spent all the funding for the ten-year rearmament plan, and also because of the recession (1900–1) following the Sino-Japanese War, it was no longer possible to issue navy bonds, and therefore there was no other way to raise capital except by continuing with high levels of taxation.

The House of Representatives, because it opposed increases in military expenditure by prolonging high levels of taxation, forced the dissolution of the Diet in December 1902. But at the general elections in March of the next year, the electorate gave 70 per cent of the seats to the *Seiyūkai* and *Kenseihontō* (the *Shinpotō* tendency within the former *Kenseitō*) which opposed the continuation of high taxation levels. In terms of votes cast also, the two parties together won 70 per cent of the total. Just a year before that war, about 70 per cent of electors (about 820,000), who were mostly agricultural landlords, were demanding a reduction in the land tax, and opposed naval rearmament.

In the shaping of a 'no war' argument during the Russo-Japanese War, the socialist Kōtoku Shūsui and the poetess Yosano Akiko are famous, but the bulk of Japanese people immediately before the outbreak of the war were war-weary at the very least.

The Katsura Cabinet, which knew that continuation of high tax levels was impossible, calculated that it could expand the navy through ordinary expenditure, and the leaders of the *Seiyūkai*, including Itō Hirobumi and Hara Kei, while maintaining their positions on the raising of finance, suppressed the opposing argument and only agreed with it on the question of naval rearmament. The House of Representatives, suffering from war weariness, was only prepared to endorse a 'Strong Country'.[7]

6

From the Russo-Japanese War to the First World War

Struggle between 'Empire' and 'Constitution'

Going to war with powerful Russia

The characteristics of Japan over the thirteen years from victory in the Russo-Japanese War (September 1905) to the ending of the First World War (November 1918) are the very essence of this book. Let us begin by examining how 'Empire' developed.

First of all, I want to give a simple explanation of how it came about that Japan went to war with such a powerful country as Russia.

Russia took advantage of the 1900 uprising in the north of China (the Boxer Rebellion) in order to despatch troops to suppress the rebellion, which was fostering an anti-foreign movement within China, and even when the rebellion had been overcome, Russia left a large force of several tens of thousands of troops in Manchuria, which was Chinese territory. Thus in actual fact, the Russians not only continued their occupation but also by signing a secret agreement with China they gave signs of moving south. As a result Japan, which aimed to place Hanguk (Korea) under its control, ended up confronting Russia (in 1897 the Lee dynasty changed the name of the country from Chosun [Chōsen in Japanese] to Hanguk [Kankoku in Japanese]).

Japan, instead of recognizing Russian rights, and de facto right of control over Manchuria, was continuing negotiations aiming to have Russia recognize the same rights for Japan over Korea, but negotiations to secure an entente did not end satisfactorily. In February of the next year (1904) at an Imperial Council it was decided to break off negotiations with Russia and open hostilities. The army and the navy together began military operations.

The Russo-Japanese War, in terms of both military and financial power, was genuinely a total war, being fought at the cost of over 200,000 dead and wounded, and costing more than 170,000,000 yen. The army, after several months of fierce fighting, besieged Lushun (Ryōjun, Port Arthur), and in March 1905 when fighting broke out at Mukden (Hōten) producing more than 100,000 dead and wounded in the two armies taken together, Japan was victorious, but Russia still had more than enough strength to continue fighting a ground war. But it was the allied fleet under the command of Tōgō Heihachirō that rescued the army from its parlous situation, by winning a spectacular victory over Russia's Baltic fleet at the Battle of the Japan Sea. As a result, the Russo-Japanese War came to a final conclusion, and the Tsar of Russia, Nicholas II, subsequently agreed to a peace conference through the good offices of the United States. Russia, however, still had enough military strength left to refuse categorically to cede territory or pay reparations.

The peace conference began in August at Portsmouth, a military port in the eastern United States. On 5 September, the Japanese plenipotentiary, Foreign Minister Komura Jūtarō, and the Russian plenipotentiary, Witte, signed the Japan–Russia Peace Treaty (the Portsmouth Treaty). As to its contents, not one penny was taken in reparations, and the Japanese demand for Sakhalin (Karafuto) to be ceded to them was shaved down so that Japan only obtained the southern half of that island. Thus the expectations of the Japanese people – who had not been informed about the country's insufficient military strength and lack of ability to continue the war, but had been fed a Diet of successive battles and successive victories – had been completely betrayed.

Nevertheless, as a result of this treaty, Japan received Lushun (Ryōjun) and Dalian (Dairen), which it coveted, as well as areas nearby over which Russia had held leasehold rights, as well as the southern part of the Eastern China Railway (between Changchun and Lushun), and it had also forced Russia to recognize Korea as a de facto Japanese protectorate. It had become an 'Empire' with special exclusive rights over Korea and north-eastern China.

Korea becoming a protectorate, and the partition of Manchuria

Before the Russo-Japanese War, however much the Constitution referred to 'The Great Japanese Imperial Constitution', Japan was neither a 'Great Japan' nor an 'Empire'. Korea was still an independent state, and the so-called rights to Manchuria and Mongolia in southern Manchuria did not belong to Japan.

By contrast Japan after the Russo-Japanese War, as we have already seen, had forced Russia to cede to it the leasehold territories of southern Manchuria centred on Lushun (Ryōjun) and Dalian (Dairen), as well as the railway, and the colonization of Korea amounted to 'Empire'. For the Japanese government, and even for the Japanese people, this meant a great change to the foreign policy conducted since the Meiji Restoration.

The view of both bureaucrats and ordinary people around the period of the Sino-Japanese War was in favour of the 'Independence of Korea'. Before the Russo-Japanese War, to this was added 'The Integrity of China'. The suppression of the Boxer Rebellion, followed by resistance to the Russian occupation of Manchuria, relates to this.

Nevertheless, in the declaration of war against Russia on 10 February 1904, the expression 'Independence of Korea' was changed to 'Integrity of Korea', and in turn the phrase 'Integrity of China' had been erased. The Russian occupation of Manchuria was not seen as impermissible from the perspective of the integrity of China, but because it endangered the 'integrity of Korea', it was seen as unacceptable.

The change from 'Independence of Korea' to 'Integrity of Korea' was not merely a question of words. In a cabinet resolution on 31 May, a mere four months after the outbreak of war, it was judged unclear whether Korea had the capacity to defend its independence over a long period, and therefore Japan 'should politically, militarily and in economic terms, gradually consolidate its foothold in that country'. The integrity of Korea did not mean the maintenance of its independence, but its conversion to the status of a protectorate.

Japan, victorious over Russia in the war, made independent Korea its protectorate, and partitioned Manchuria with Russia, though Manchuria was supposed to be integrated into China. It was the government and the ordinary people of China that became most indignant at this. Japan, which ten years earlier had begun a war proclaiming a 'Liberation of Korea', was now unambiguously aiming to make Korea its colony, and Japan, which fostered expectations among the government and people of China calling for the integrity of China, had portioned with Russia the rights and benefits of Manchuria, which was Chinese territory.

What Japan was especially concerned about after the Russo-Japanese War was probable demands for the return of Manchuria from the government and the people of China incensed at Japanese duplicity. In fact after Japan had won the Sino-Japanese and then the Russo-Japanese Wars, China did not immediately demand the return of Manchuria. On the contrary the Chinese government once again concluded a treaty with Japan in December 1905. This included the cession, promised to Japan in the Sino-Japanese Peace Treaty, of the leasehold rights to Lushun (Ryōjun), Dalian (Dairen) and later the southern part of the eastern China Railway, which was to become the Mantetsu (south Manchurian Railway), as well as coalfields and other facilities attached to it (this was the Japan–China Treaty concerning Manchuria, commonly known as the Peking Treaty).

The Imperial Defence Policy

Within the Japanese government, however, Yamagata Aritomo, elder statesman and chief of the general staff, understood fairly well that the Chinese rulers had signed this treaty without having a full understanding of it. He feared intensely that in the future China would press for the return of Japan's special rights in Manchuria.

On 19 February 1907, having obtained the agreement of the Conference of five star military officers, the 'Imperial Defence Policy' was submitted to the Emperor, and was well known for the following phrase: 'Those that should be regarded as future enemies include Russia as number one, and then America, Germany and France.' The army regarded Russia and France, and the navy regarded America and Germany, as important potential enemies.[1] But to designate America, which had worked so hard to negotiate the conclusion of the Russo-Japanese War, as a potential enemy, was not only impolite but it also seems impossible that Japan at that period could have imagined the attack on Pearl Harbour at the end of 1941. Again, for the army to designate Russia as a 'future enemy', which only one and a half years before had fought a war with Japan that was close to being a total war, was rather unnatural. To designate all the major powers of Europe and America as 'future enemies', except for Great Britain, was something that exceeded Japanese power.

According to research by Kadota Jun, Lieutenant-Colonel Tanaka Giichi, member of the General Staff Headquarters, drafted a proposal titled 'Imperial Defence Policy', in which he wrote: 'It is almost out of the question that America would invade our territory and commit aggression against us, and we are not going to set out to attack the United States.'[2] If no plans whatsoever existed for the armies of Japan and America to attack each other, there was no possibility for the navies of the two countries to fight each other. For Tanaka, the idea that the Japanese Navy might designate the United States as a 'potential enemy' stretched credibility.

And so, was it realistic to think that the army might regard Russia as a 'potential enemy'? What the 'Imperial Defence Policy' established was that since the armed forces of Japan and Russia had fought to the death for a year and a half, the current situation was only eighteen months after the end of that war, and for both officials and ordinary people it was clear that there was no desire to fight a war again. I think that at such a time, the idea that the army was preparing for a Russian war of revenge, and was suggesting in writing that Russia was a 'potential enemy', was just as unrealistic as the notion that the navy in the Pacific Ocean would fight a decisive battle with the American fleet. For the army, their true potential enemies were surely elsewhere.

Where were the *real* potential enemies?

The 'statement of opinion' with which Yamagata had petitioned the Emperor before his 'Imperial Defence Policy' of 1907, was something he had put forward in October of the previous year as his 'private view', or his own statement of opinion, and he replied directly to these doubts about it. He cited China as just as much of a 'potential enemy' as Russia. In the 'Imperial Defence Policy' that received the formal approval of the Emperor four months later, 'Russia, Germany, America and France were cited as "potential enemies", but in Yamagata's "private opinion" this designation was restricted to Russia and China. America, Germany and France were not included'. In considering the complex relations with Russia, Germany and France, Yamagata expressed himself in the following manner:

> The most important enemy to be identified in our strategic plan is Russia, and there is no need to regard other major European powers as enemies and prepare against them.[3]

From this we can see that among the four 'potential enemies' listed in the 'Imperial Defence Policy', America, Germany and France had dropped off the list, and in their stead China had been newly added:

> We must never forget that China must be added as the second enemy after Russia.[4]

Why should China become a hypothetical enemy for Japan?

It goes without saying that as a result of the Russo-Japanese War, Japan now controlled special interests in Lushun (Ryōjun) and Dalian (Dairen), both being in southern Manchuria (Kwantung Province) within an area of Chinese sovereignty.

Even today from time to time we hear stories about how Japanese victory in the Russo-Japanese War, as a victory of coloured peoples over white-skinned peoples, energized Asian peoples as far away as India. In one sense the Elder Statesman Yamagata Aritomo understood things in this fashion. But in fact there was a big difference between later Asianist discourse and the way Yamagata saw it, in that he considered that the focus of coloured peoples was not necessarily directed towards white-skinned peoples. The gist of his argument was as follows:

> We have fought and defeated Russia, but China, which up to the present has feared Russia above all, while making light of white-skinned peoples, confidently hopes to maintain its independence by its own power, and they are raising their voices in their attempt to regain their rights. Even the Peking Government, which was stubborn in its determination to retain ancient practices, has now promised to move towards a constitutional system, and is enthusiastically discussing reform of the bureaucracy. After that they will go on to reform their taxation system, and are in the early stages of establishing a proper military system, so that they are becoming an enemy that ought not to be underestimated.
>
> This being the case, the Peking Government will attempt first of all to damage our rights in Manchuria, and there is a danger that this will provoke a serious clash. In particular, when the Kwantung lease agreement reaches its term (1923), China will certainly demand Japanese withdrawal, but since Japan from the beginning is not able to accede to this demand, it is quite possible that negotiations will break down and war may break out.
>
> The Japanese strategic plan must treat China as the second most important enemy.[5]

This address to the Throne of October 1906 occurred less than a year after the Chinese government had been pressured into recognizing, in December 1905, the special rights to southern Manchuria handed over in the Russo-Japanese Peace Treaty. To worry about 1923 – the year in which the time limit for handing back the territories would elapse – appears somewhat neurotic. However, with the declaration of war on Russia, the policy had been suddenly changed to asserting 'the integrity of Korea', and Japan, which had previously proclaimed 'the independence of Korea and integrity of China', now with its victory in war had made Korea its dependency and had divided up Manchuria with Russia – in these circumstances Yamagata, as one of the Japanese leaders, was perhaps experiencing disquiet.

The 1923 crisis

Nevertheless, over a full forty years of Japanese history from the end of the Russo-Japanese War in 1905 up to the defeat in 1945, 'rights and privileges in Manchuria' were always regarded as a natural 'lifeline', but at first, surprisingly, were only going to last for eighteen years up to 1923. If the notorious 'Twenty-one Demands' to China had not been made in 1915, then during the international popularity of 'self-determination' following the First World War, who knows whether or not restoration of the special rights and privileges in Manchuria that were coming to an end in 1923 would have been rejected.

As I shall explain later on, I am critical of the outdated 'imperialist diplomacy' argument, according to which Japan took advantage of a political vacuum in East Asia, like a robber taking advantage of a house on fire, in order to force China to extend to ninety-nine years of Japanese rights and privileges in Manchuria by means of the twenty-one demands. However, when we consider that from the standpoint of 1915, Japan's 'rights and privileges in Manchuria and Mongolia' had only eight years to run, even if use of force motivated by greed, such as the twenty-one demands, was out of the question, it seems difficult to imagine that any statesman of that period during a great war would have resisted the temptation to force the Chinese government to accept some extension of the period of validity.

My understanding of this may perhaps reflect rigidity of thought of a kind into which a historian is apt to fall. A historical researcher understands the course of events as the continuation of a time series. Today follows yesterday, and today will continue tomorrow.

When it is a normal period, this kind of understanding will probably hit the mark. Of course, seen from a historical point of view, when judging standards for good and evil, a different perspective is possible. If you judge decisively that it was mistaken for Japan, inebriated with its victory in the Russo-Japanese War, to obtain special rights in southern Manchuria, then you do not need to examine in detail the 'Imperial Defence Policy' that had fixed this mistake in place. According to this argument, if Japan in the Russo-Japanese War had not taken over the 'special rights and privileges in southern Manchuria' and then worried that China would take them back, the need for China to be designated in the Defence Policy as the second-most important (but hidden) hypothetical enemy would have disappeared, and the twenty-one demands would have been unnecessary.

On the other hand, if we do not judge history like a prosecutor, we cannot so easily dismiss Yamagata's '1923 crisis'. Since the special rights and privileges in southern Manchuria handed over by Russia to Japan were from the very beginning limited to eighteen years, then if he definitely judged that in 1923 these rights should be handed back, the historical analysis [described above] falls apart.

Is there no way of resolving this dilemma? Even though immediately after the Russo-Japanese War Yamagata expressed strong disquiet at the time limit placed on Japan's special rights and privileges in Manchuria and Mongolia, and in this we have to acknowledge a degree of clear foresight on his part, was he really unable to criticize the twenty-one demands? Does not the viewpoint of historians change depending on whether it is a normal period or a world-historical time of change? Before and after a great period of global change such as the First World War, the operation of 'Empire' would change fundamentally. It was unclear whether the situation before the Great War, in which the advanced countries could divide up special rights and privileges in China among themselves, would continue after the Great War. In such a situation, Yamagata's reconsidered argument about 'a 1923 crisis' was probably necessary. I think that we need to investigate the twenty-one demands issued right in the middle of the Great War in 1915 from a perspective different from that of the 'Imperial Defence Policy' written after the Russo-Japanese War.

Naval stratagems

Let us return to the 'Imperial Defence Policy'. As I have already pointed out, among the 'potental enemies' proposed by the army top brass, including Tanaka Giichi, Yamagata Aritomo and others, America, Germany and France were not included.

As is well known from the Yellow Sea Naval War (September 1894) and the Japan Sea Naval War (May 1905), the contribution of the Japan Sea forces in the Sino-Japanese and Russo-Japanese Wars was enormous. However, as a result of the Russo-Japanese War, for Japan, which made Korea its protectorate and placed southern Manchuria under its control, the main forces defending this territory were Japan's Korean Army and the Kwantung Army, while the role of the navy was subordinate. If Yamagata Aritomo and others like him regarded Russia and China as potential enemies, then few chances of action would be given to the navy.

As we have already seen, the navy, opposing this, succeeded in adding the United States and Germany as 'potential enemies'. As a result, in the 'Imperial

Defence Policy' presented to the Emperor in 1907 in the joint names of the chiefs of staff (in the navy's case the chief of Military Command), the army specified twenty-five divisions as the norm, while the navy specified eight warships of the latest design, and eight armoured cruisers.[6]

Given that the number of divisions in the Japanese Army immediately after the Russo-Japanese War was seventeen, it followed that twenty-five divisions meant an increase of eight. Moreover, for the navy, 'of the latest design' meant warships no more than eight years old. Since the warship construction planned before the Russo-Japanese War, the plan had been fulfilled to the extent that after the war four warships and four armoured cruisers had been constructed, the 8.8 plan (eight warships and eight armoured cruisers) amounted to twice the number actually built. This meant that four extra warships and four armoured cruisers were purchased later.

Incidentally, the navy as such was a real money-gobbler. Four years later, the four pre-war vessels were no longer 'of the latest design', and it was necessary to buy four new vessels. Four years after the Imperial Defence Policy was given the seal of approval, meaning in 1911, and also in the following year of 1912, the movement operating under the slogan 'Overthrow that domain-clique government, defend constitutionalism' emerged within the Diet and outside it. Four years later was 1915, and in the year before that (as I shall discuss in more detail further on), the government, which aimed to increase naval spending, was overthrown as the result of a popular movement incensed by corruption in the navy. The fact that this movement both inside and outside the Diet (often lumped together as the 'Taishō Political Change') was active at the same time as the replacement of warships 'of the latest design' appears not to have been coincidental.

Moreover, it is well known that the chance presented to this movement wishing to 'overthrow the domain clique government' lay in the independent resignation of the army minister, Uehara Yūsaku, who was earnestly demanding that two divisions should be completed out of the six divisions left uncompleted as part of the twenty-five-division regime that was being created.

We shall not make 'War' but we shall pursue 'Rearmament'

As these things demonstrate, the great expansion plan for the army and navy, which had been strengthened by victory in the Russo-Japanese War (as I shall describe in the next chapter), met strong resistance from those promoting

'Constitution domestically'. But first of all there is one more thing we need to recognize. The Imperial Defence Policy aimed to maintain and strengthen the 'Japanese Empire' that had only just been born, but it did not carry the intention of fighting an actual war.

After the Russo-Japanese War, Russia, pursuing a southward strategy into East Asia, surprisingly found itself in harmony with Japan. In the first Japan–Russia Agreement signed in July 1907, the first article of its secret agreement gave mutual recognition of the special rights and privileges that both countries held in north and south Manchuria.

The Japanese government, including the army and navy, cooperating with Russia, sought to defend the special rights and privileges that they had extracted from China and divided them up among themselves, so that a recurrence of war between Japan and Russia was out of the question. This was only an excuse for an army rearmament. Moreover, even concerning the '1923 crisis' about which Yamagata Aritomo had warned (the expiry of the special rights and privileges extracted from Russia), even if the army were to increase its military strength in Korea and southern Manchuria, the possibility of this leading to a revival of war between Japan and China was negligible. So long as the Japanese side did not engage in military action designed to expand its rights in Manchuria and Mongolia, the danger of war with China hardly existed. Of course, the idea of risking a showdown between the Japanese and US navies in the Pacific was probably absent from the minds of the Japanese naval top brass at that time.

Putting this in different terms, the fact that the army had designated Russia, and the navy the United States, as potential enemies, meant in effect that Japan had decided not to go to war at that time. But the strengthened Japanese armed forces might well increase the possibility of aggression or advance into East Asia. Yamagata's argument placing China as a potential enemy demonstrated this. The real meaning of the Imperial Defence Policy drawn up in 1907 was that 'we will engage in aggression but not in war, we will not go to war, but we will work to rearm'.

Resistance to Taishō democracy and compromise with it

The twenty years between the movement opposing the peace treaty straight after the Russo-Japanese War (September 1905) and the granting of universal male suffrage (1925) are called the period of 'Taishō democracy'. The period broadly overlaps with the previously discussed period of empire, of 'we will engage in aggression but not in war'. It was exactly the period of 'Constitution domestically, Empire externally'. As I set out in the Introduction to Part II, the leading researcher into Taishō democracy, who criticized its limitations, was the late Matsuo Takayoshi, Emeritus Professor of Kyoto University. He made clear that 'in criticising aggression against Korea and China, Yoshino Sakuzō was – to put it strongly – isolated and without assistance'.

In other words, it can be said that Taishō democracy closed its eyes to aggression and aimed to bring about party politics and universal suffrage ('Constitution domestically').

But just like the 'Constitution' forces before the Sino-Japanese War and the Russo-Japanese War, Taishō democracy also strongly opposed rearmament. So far as this is concerned (and I deal with this later in more detail), when we consider the question at the end of 1912 of expanding the army by two divisions, and the Siemens corruption scandal in March 1914, it is easy to speculate about this.

In fact, this had its origin in attempts to manage the situation following the Russo-Japanese War, which, just like managing the situation after the Sino-Japanese War, began with agreement between the cabinet and the Diet concerning rearmament. The cabinet that followed the Russo-Japanese War was the first Saionji Kinmochi Cabinet, based on the *Seiyūkai* Party in the House of Representatives, established in January 1906. This being the case, financial policy, including financing of army and navy rearmament, probably reflected the constraints imposed upon the government by the House of Representatives, through that party in the year after the war. The budget, however, had been finalized in broad outline in December of the previous year, so that all the Diet session, that began the next year, could do was to reject the budget as a whole (meaning that the budget of the previous year would have come into force), or promote minor amendments.

The first Saionji Cabinet, in order to assuage popular disquiet over the no-compensation peace treaty with Russia the previous year, made itself into a party cabinet with the *Seiyūkai* president as prime minister. In this way there was no need to fear a rejection of the government's budget by the House of Representatives. Since, however, the cabinet was established in January 1906, when the cabinet began, the broad outline of the budget had already been determined by the first Katsura Cabinet, which was a non-party cabinet dependent exclusively upon military and civilian bureaucrats.

According to research conducted by Nakazato Yūji, the budget as a parting present from this military clique and civilian bureaucrat government included continuous funding of army and navy rearmament, beginning with the establishment of four extra army divisions.[7] On this point, there is some similarity to management following the Sino-Japanese War, but managing the situation after the Russo-Japanese War, known for its peace treaty without compensation, was far briefer, and the Imperial Defence Policy, discussed earlier in some detail, of course did not include continuous funding. For this reason, the House of Representatives was not able to impose constraints upon the government.

Iaku jōsō – Did the Imperial Defence Policy without cabinet recognition have no influence?

Moreover, so far as this policy was concerned, the army chief of the general staff and the navy chief of military command (in this book I refer to the army and navy chiefs of the General Staff) had direct access to the Emperor without obtaining the agreement of the cabinet, and they received Imperial agreement. The fact that both chiefs of the General Staff could approach the Emperor without going through the cabinet was known as *iaku jōsō*. Both 'i' and 'aku' mean 'curtain' (tobari), to indicate that the Emperor as Field Marshall directed the war by holding a strategy meeting 'inside the curtain'. This of course is the derivation of the term, whereas the actual *jōsō* was held in the Imperial Palace.*

This *iaku jōsō*, as its derivation implies, shows that there was no constitutional doubt about the acceptance of the Emperor's power of command (limited to strategy and tactics). Article 11 of the Meiji Constitution states: 'The Emperor has the supreme command of the Army and Navy.'

On the other hand, whether *iaku jōsō* was valid in decisions concerning the Emperor's power of 'organization' given in article 12 was a divisive issue. The power of organization, meaning the organization of the army and navy, and the peace standing of the army and navy, was in the hands of the Emperor's government, and interference in this by the Diet was forbidden. Concerning the interpretation of this phrase, the explanation by Itō Hirobumi in his *Commentaries on the Constitution* itself pointed both ways. Itō wrote: 'This basically means that the relevant minister assists the Throne, and as with access to the Emperor for the Military Command, supreme power belongs to His Majesty, but he must not wait for Diet interference.'

---

* Translator's note: The fact that the author needs to explain this term to Japanese readers perhaps indicates that such a practice now appears completely outdated.

'Lectures on the Constitution', by Minobe Tatsukichi, was published five years after the Imperial Defence Policy was drawn up, and became the mainstream approach among academics and also among government officials between the Taishō period and the beginning of the Shōwa period. Among his interpretations of Itō, one phrase that he ignored was: 'as with the access to the Emperor of the military High Command.' If this was the case, Itō's interpretation was: 'Basically the relevant minister assists the Throne, . . . Supreme power belongs to His Majesty, but he must not wait for Diet interference.' In other words, decisions on 'the organisation and peace standing of the Army and Navy' required the assistance of 'the relevant minister' – in other words assistance by the army minister and the navy minister was required, and no interference from the Diet would be allowed. Thus, this was Minobe's interpretation of Itō's explanation, as well as his explanation of article 12 of the Constitution.

The Imperial Defence Policy undoubtedly came under the rubric of 'the organisation and peace standing of the Army and Navy'. According to Minobe's interpretation, since an address to the Emperor by the chief of the general staff and the navy chief of military command would not be sufficient to satisfy the requirements of article 12, it would have no binding force as a national policy. According to Kadota Jun, and in documents of the Defence Agency's (later Ministry) Defence Research Bureau Office on the History of War, after the Emperor accepted the address to the Throne, Saionji Kinmochi received from the Emperor a message apologizing for the lateness of his reply, but there is no record of a report having been made to the prime minister through the army and navy chiefs of staff, nor is there a record concerning the Imperial Defence Policy in the cabinet, the Defence Ministry or the Navy Ministry, he says.[8]

Thus if we ask whether the Imperial Defence Policy and related matters were just a private promise between the chiefs of staff of the army and navy, together with the Emperor, and therefore had no impact on the national policy, this was not the only issue involved. As I wrote earlier, Minobe's interpretation of article 12 only worked by ignoring the section from Itō Hirobumi's *Commentaries on the Constitution* (the same in effect as the prerogative of the Supreme Command to have direct access to the Emperor). If he did not ignore this section, then since decisions on defence policy belonged 'to the Supreme Power of the Emperor in the same way as privileged access to the Emperor', then the difference from the independence of the Supreme Command prerogative in article 11 disappeared. According to this interpretation, in both cases the Supreme Command could appeal to the Throne without consulting with the cabinet.

Leaving aside these vexatious issues of constitutional interpretation and moving to a conclusion, concerning decisions on defence policy as stipulated in article 12, the chiefs of staff of the army and navy had about the same degree of power as the minister of war and the minister of the navy. In a word, the 'Imperial Defence Policy' decided in 1907 possessed some validity even against the cabinet.

Positive policy and rearmament

Just as at any other time, however, if your long-sleeved coat has no sleeve, you cannot wave it about. Even if the plan for twenty-five army divisions, and for the eight by eight fleet were accepted, Saionji Kinmochi, as prime minister, being constrained by financial difficulties in the aftermath of a total war, asked the Emperor to respect the cabinet's approach in effecting what would happen and when. When the Emperor accepted the 'Imperial Defence Policy', confrontation between the military and the cabinet over the extent and speed of rearmament had already begun.

Standing in the way of the continuing expenses that remained unpaid were not only the prerogatives of the cabinet. After the Russo-Japanese War, whether the current party was in power, or even when it was out of power, the *Seiyūkai* 'positive (development) policies', which also stood in the way of the army and navy rearmament, were a great and continuing influence on budget decision-making. As I have already pointed out, the *Seiyūkai*, ever since the final period of the *Jiyūtō* that had preceded it, promoted the spread to the provinces of transport and communication infrastructure, including railways, harbours, telegraph and telephone, by which it cemented its local political base. What was involved was a shift from *minryoku kyūyō* (reducing the people's burdens) to *sekkyokushugi* (positive development policies). The *Seiyūkai* obtained a majority in the House of Representatives in the general elections of 1908, and thus became the party in power, but from before that it was continuously the largest party promoting the same policies.

As I have already made clear when discussing the 'Constitution', a budget could not be put in place while ignoring the approach of the leading party in the House of Representatives. Thus the leading party continued to budget for infrastructure improvements second only to the self-financing of expenditure on the army and navy.

As part of this, and as shown by the expression *gaden intetsu* (bring the railway to my fields), the extension of railways was its sharpest tool in the task of persuading electors. About half a century ago, when I was researching materials concerning the politician Sugita Teiichi of Fukui Prefecture during the Meiji period, I heard the following anecdote from the owner of an old local farmhouse: 'a bridge means one generation, but a railway means three generations.' If a politician manages to get a railway extended to the district, his base of support will be secure down to the grandchildren's generation.

The first Saionji Cabinet in 1906, based on the *Seiyūkai* as party in power, introduced a bill to issue government bonds as capital with which the State could purchase seventeen private railways over ten years. Just buying private railways whose management had been poor and creating the National Railways, thus 'bringing the railway to my fields', was not enough. But this legislation to nationalize the railways was the signal for expansion of the National Railways, and made *Seiyūkai* supporters very happy.

The railway nationalization law was passed in March 1906, and the 'Imperial Defence Policy' in February 1907. Within a year and a half after the end of the Russo-Japanese War, plans were drawn up for major expansion of both the railways and for the army and navy.

As I have already pointed out, Prime Minister Saionji, who had been shown the 'Imperial Defence Policy' by the Emperor, understood it as a long-term objective, but because of the tight financial situation following the war replied to the Emperor that he would like him to honour the Diet's views so far as the timing of implementation was concerned. The cabinet had already implemented railway nationalization by financing it with government bonds. To this it added the army and navy rearmament based on the defence policy. From a novice's perspective it looked as though the national finances were approaching bankruptcy.

Certainly the financial difficulties after the Russo-Japanese War were out of the ordinary. War expenses over more than a year and a half of total war were close to six times the general account expenditure prior to the war, at 1,700,000,000 yen. About 700 million of this consisted of foreign loans, 600 million consisted of domestic loans, and the remaining more than 300 million was raised from taxation, including a special tax rise. About 1,300,000,000 yen of foreign loans were medium-term loans, and all of them would have to be paid back with interest. The 320,000,000 yen special tax rise yielded twice the pre-war tax revenue of 150,000,000 yen.

As for the economic management following the Russo-Japanese War, it developed on the basis of a 1,300,000,000 yen loan and increased taxation close to the limit of what the taxpayer could bear (the special tax was not abolished with the termination of the war). Increasing taxation beyond this level was impossible, and so when we consider that making use of the 1,300,000,000 loan, on this basis nationalizing the railways, creating twenty-five army divisions (meaning an increase of eight divisions) and an eight/eight fleet (meaning an increase of four for each of the two categories), it is extraordinary that by the final year of the Meiji era (1912), Japan had not become bankrupt.

The Katsura–Saionji system – the Katsura bureaucratic clique plus the army versus the Saionji Seiyūkai plus the navy

If it had only been a question of conflict over tax increases between the army, the navy and the *Seiyūkai*, financial difficulties would not just have resulted in immediate political turmoil. The political system following the Russo-Japanese War is usually called the 'Katsura–Saionji system'. The name derived from the fact that Katsura Tarō, representing the bureaucratic clique that controlled the military, the bureaucracy and the House of Peers on the one hand, and Saionji Kinmochi, the president of the *Seiyūkai*, which held about half the seats in the House of Representatives on the other hand, alternated in the position of prime minister, and sought to maintain harmony between the two sides. The renowned journalist Tokutomi Sohō, in 1916, not long after the system came to an end, painted the following picture of it in his book:

> We are safe in calling the period of about ten years between 1903 and 1912 as the Katsura-Saionji period. When Katsura formed a cabinet, Saionji, who ran the *Seiyūkai*, assisted it in the House of Representatives, and when Saionji formed a cabinet, Katsura, together with what we may call the party in power having a majority in the House of Peers, helped it along.... In this way calm was maintained over a period of ten years in domestic politics.
> But when we have a scenario like this where the central of politics run smoothly, there is nothing difficult in the world; there is nothing as pleasant as politics ... and the most easygoing people may specialise in it with an untroubled mind.[9]

As we may deduce from the latter part of this quotation, the intention of Tokutomi Sohō's book was to analyse the conflicts between the various forces excluded from politics within the two camps and by the two camps, which developed in the background of superficial calm. If there had not been conflict from these excluded elements, the process of political reconstruction known as the 'Taishō Political Change', which we shall discuss later, might never have occurred just as a result of financial difficulties.

In the bureaucratic clique directed by Katsura Tarō, who came from an army background, the interests of the navy, which showed little concern for rights and privileges in Manchuria and Mongolia, were not taken seriously, and instead the navy moved closer to Saionji as head of the *Seiyūkai*. The army, the bureaucracy and the House of Peers were under the influence of Katsura Tarō, while the navy and the House of Representatives placed their expectations on Saionji Kinmochi, so that the Katsura–Saionji system maintained a balance between these forces.

Looked at in this way, the Katsura–Saionji system, which lasted seven years from the formation of the first Saionji Cabinet after the Russo-Japanese War until the final year of the Meiji era (1912), or what I have titled the '1900 political system' in a previous publication,[10] did not appear to differ greatly from the political system that existed from the inauguration of the Diet in 1890. The most important work of politics was to reconcile the interests of the army and navy with those of the *Jiyūtō* (later *Seiyūkai*) representing the interests of rural landlords. It was not easy to reconcile the interests of 'Empire' with those of 'Constitution'. But forces concerned with such reconciliation were rather small.

The emergence of urban commerce and industry

The political structure, however, changed greatly after the Russo-Japanese War, and the issues of politics were no longer confined to reconciling interests between the army and navy on the one hand and agricultural landlords on the other hand. Along with the progress of urbanization, those working in commerce and industry, as well as those in various city occupations, had begun to press their individual demands.

With the political emergence of commercial and industrial interests, they participated in general election campaigns and engaged in pressure group activities.

The first development came about through revision of the election law. Under the second Yamagata government in March 1900, by means of revision enacted after receiving support from the *Kenseitō* (a semi-government party), 73 out of 376 (later 379) electoral seats were separated from local area (*gun*) seats and were distributed to independent seats in cities. The government committee member Kaneko Kentarō (minister of agriculture and commerce) asserted: 'we shall elect to the House of Representatives those representing commerce and industry comparable in number with those representing agriculture.'[11]

But with 73 seats out of 379, the political influence of urban commerce and industry was not particularly great. Their influence was rather exercised through pressure groups.

It was in 1892 that Chambers of Commerce formed an association, which acquired the status of an association from its third congress, when it joined the Tokyo Chamber of Commerce. The nationalization of business tax in 1896 gave it the opportunity to behave as a pressure group at the association of Chambers of Commerce. Business tax as a local tax varied up and down between prefectures, and made a unified movement to reduce the tax problem. This nationalization of the tax system on the one hand meant increases to tax rates, but by uniting in an association of Chambers of Commerce at the local level, a movement to reduce tax rates became possible.

With a special tax levied during the Russo-Japanese War of 1904–5, business tax had increased 4.5 times and was continued after the war had finished, so that demands from the association of Chambers of Commerce became stronger. In particular, the Russo-Japanese War panic from the end of 1907 stimulated pressure activity by the association. When the first Saionji government based on the *Seiyūkai* sought to overcome a funding deficit by a tax on saké and a consumption tax on sugar, as well as introducing an oil consumption tax, the association, anxious about low consumption, started to work in conjunction with tax rise victims including small-scale manufacturers and city dwellers. In January of the following year, marking the inauguration of the Tokyo Chamber of Commerce, its acting Chairman, Nakano Buei (president of the Tokyo Chamber of Commerce), spoke as follows:

> Concerning this question, the Government persists in sticking to its own policy. In order to stop this in its tracks, by petitioning government people, or making representations to them, we can never attain our purposes, and this is clear from the beginning. There is nothing for it but to use the power of the Japanese people.

If we turn this round, the demands of the Chamber of Commerce were only to 'petition' the government, or make 'representations' to it. 'To use the power of the Japanese people' was an overly bombastic expression, but just the fact that this Chamber of Commerce Association was not only addressing the government but also appealing to public opinion, made sense. It is true that there were differences between extending railways to local areas (positive policies) and reducing land tax. But the important point about politics up to that point is that, rather than considering the demands of rural landlords, attention now had to be given to reducing business tax and abolishing tax on consumption, in other words to the demands of small and medium commercial and industrial forms in cities.

The pluralization of conflicts of interest

Obviously the financial world that occupied the core of the Japanese economy did not depend upon 'the power of the Japanese people'. But in the midst of the panic that began at the end of 1907, financial enterprises that had purchased government bonds during the war pressed the government to redeem them quickly. Omitting details and going straight to the conclusion, banks wanted redemption of wartime loans, small and medium firms desired business tax to be reduced, and very small firms wished for abolition of tax on consumers, while ordinary city dwellers suffering from rising prices supported them.

From the viewpoint of government financial policy, there was only one way to respond to this situation, namely to trim the bureaucracy and tighten financial policy. If they did this, however, not only for army and navy rearmament but also for infrastructure investment by the ruling *Seiyūkai* party, a brake would have to be applied. They needed to meet the demands of the army, the navy, the *Seiyūkai*, the financial world as well as small and medium industries. But Japan had not received a penny of reparations following the Russo-Japanese War, and so if they did all this the national finances would probably at once face bankruptcy. The general magazine *Nihon oyobi Nihonjin* (Japan and the Japanese) for the final year of Meiji (1912) painted a broad-brush picture of the conflicted situation of different interests, divided in all directions:[12]

> Speaking without restraint, our society today is so selfish and irresponsible that we are astounded. Does nobody among our sixty million compatriots understand the difficulties of our imperial finances? But though they understand what a poor state our finances are in, bureaucrats compete to expand the projects for which they are responsible. At present the Army is fiercely demanding an increase in the number of its divisions, while the Navy demands that the number of warships be increased. When we consider that bankers are demanding the redemption of government loans, that the business world wants a bonanza of new projects, and that people in general demand tax reductions, those representing the majority of the people (the *Seiyūkai*) take on all sorts of local interest issues, and either demand railway extensions, or repairs to harbours and rivers. Even knowing that consultations on these issues are impossible, everybody is in competition with each other demanding an impossible level of consultation. This is the current situation.[13]

Progress of the democratization movement

The explosion of individual demands to favour their interests by different social groups was disadvantageous to 'Imperialism', but advantageous to 'Democratization'. Up to the Russo-Japanese War, interests only needed to be reconciled between the army and navy on the one hand and agricultural landlords on the other hand, but once the tax threshold for the right to vote was lowered, and the number of electors doubled from 500,000 to 1,000,000, this was the limit of progress towards democracy. At that time the electoral law targeted males over 25, but even using this definition, the number of adult males was more than 10 million (at the general elections of 1928, the first when all males over the age of 25 had the right to vote, the number of electors was about 12,500,000).

Following the Russo-Japanese War, the electoral law which accorded the right to vote to those paying at least 10 yen in direct national taxes, of at least 25 years of age and of male gender, remained unchanged until in March 1919, when the tax threshold was lowered to 3 yen in direct national taxes and the universal male suffrage law was not implemented until 1925.

Despite the emergence of proliferating confrontation between interest groups mentioned earlier, there was no call for universal male suffrage until the outbreak of the First World War in August 1914. The main reason for this was that the goal of progressive political parties and intellectuals was focused on getting rid of cabinets monopolized by domain-cliques ('transcendental cabinets' that excluded political parties), and establishing party cabinets.

Of course political progress is something that only takes place in stages. The goal of the Popular Rights Movement around 1880 was to establish a Diet (Parliament), and then after the Diet had been put in place the goal was to establish a parliamentary cabinet system, enabling cabinets to be formed from the majority party (or parties) in the House of Representatives. It is symbolic that the slogan of the democratic movement that developed in cities throughout the country, opposed to the tyranny of the army, between the end of 1912 and February of 1913, was 'Down with the Domain-Clique, defend Constitutionalism'.

As I have noted earlier, the proliferation of organizational and group interests after the Russo-Japanese War brought about rivalries 'that could not be resolved by discussion'. To use contemporary language, this was 'politics without resolution'. But it did also have the sense of democratizing politics. In a situation where there were four or five groups having influence over policymaking, this was a step towards democracy in the sense of unravelling oligarchy. And then street demonstrations in cities that emerged after the Russo-Japanese War, receiving some support from ruling forces, brought about an expansion of the right to political expression.

The Hibiya Arson Incident in 1905 at the end of the Russo-Japanese War, followed by the first Constitution defence movement and the Siemens corruption affair in 1914 (to be discussed in the next chapter), involved gatherings of citizens and demonstrations in the cities amounting to tens of thousands of participants. This forced out of power several cabinets of the time, and greatly furthered the progress of democracy. Yoshino Sakuzō, who had just emerged as the practical theorist of Taishō democracy, in the journal *Chūō Kōron* just after the Siemens Affair, singled out three 'mass demonstration movements', 'seen from the perspective of the constitutional development of contemporary Japan . . . as a development to be applauded'. Yoshino used the word 'Constitution' in the same sense as 'Democracy', in the same way as I have used 'Constitution' in contrast to 'Empire'. Yoshino, following on from the previous quotation, explained as follows why the movement of mass demonstrations was 'a development to be applauded'.

> In the sense that the judgement of the masses controls final decisions concerning the interpretation of political issues and transfer of power, and that it gives political significance to the judgement of the masses, I believe that this is a development to be applauded.[14]

7

From the Taishō Political Change to the Siemens Affair

Stagnation of 'Empire' and Surge of 'Constitution'

Twin deficits

With victory in the Russo-Japanese War, the progress of 'Empire' in Japan rapidly increased. Acquisition of rights in southern Manchuria (1905) and the assimilation of Korea (1910) were external symbols of 'Imperialism', while the Imperial Defence Policy (1907) may be seen as its internal preparation.

This trend, however, from the assimilation of Korea in 1910, made it inevitable that the progress of 'Empire' would stall. One reason for this lay in what were termed the twin deficits, in government finance and in the balance of payments.

The special contingency tax imposed during the Russo-Japanese War was continued after the war had ended, but at the same time, in financial management after the war, it had become impossible to increase taxation apart from indirect taxation on saké and some other items. Moreover, in the raising of foreign loans, upon which the economy had become dependent during the war, those in charge of finance had become averse to such dependency. This was because the repayment of capital and interest on loans raised during the war was 600,000,000 yen (1.5 times the revenue from land tax) between 1907 and 1911. As I have already pointed out, domestic financial institutions that were demanding rapid repayment of existing loans taken out in conditions of economic recession seemed unlikely to respond favourably to the idea of raising loans domestically. Finance and credit during the Russo-Japanese War were conducted in a situation allowing little flexibility.

In such a situation, no cabinet appeared that would respond either to the army's demand that its seventeen divisions to be increased to twenty-five or to the navy's demand to purchase of four warships of the latest design and four armoured cruisers. Both the domain-clique cabinet led by Katsura Tarō and the Saionji Kinmochi Cabinet organized by the president of the *Seiyūkai* only acknowledged a part of those demands.

Specifically, all that these cabinets accepted was an increase of two army divisions, the seventeenth (Okayama) and the eighteenth (Kurume). So far as the navy's demand for an eight by eight fleet (for the time being four vessels in each category up to 1911) was concerned, the building of only one warship and three armoured cruisers was accepted (much as in the case of the army). Under the Saionji Cabinet, in the budget for 1912 (the final year of Meiji, which became the first year of Taishō), the purchase of three warships was accepted, so that putting these together with the one warship and three armoured cruisers authorized by the second Katsura cabinet that preceded it, the navy was on the way to obtaining a formation of four warships and three armoured cruisers, which was not far off its original demand.

Why was public opinion lenient towards the navy, but severe towards the army?

Why was it that naval rearmament, targeting the United States as the potential enemy – a country which in the Imperial Defence Policy was hardly seen as an adversary by the army – proceeded far more smoothly in practice than increasing the number of army divisions? Moreover, this contrast became all the more obvious under the second Saionji Cabinet organized by the president of the *Seiyūkai*, the largest party in the House of Representatives, with its authorization of three warships.

The process whereby in 1907 the Imperial Defence Policy was drawn up hints at the reasons for it. Just as Yamagata Aritomo and Tanaka Giichi of the army asserted, a war between Japan and America, envisaged by the navy, was a total fabrication. Compared with that scenario, the prospect of a war with Russia, or a war with China (especially a war with China), had a genuine ring of realism about it.

I have already mentioned that Japan, which was going ahead with the development of Manchuria and Mongolia, would face the termination of its involvement in 1923, but would not be able to return those rights to China. On the other hand, China since its defeat in the Sino-Japanese War was not simply burning with a sense of revenge against Japan, but economically, militarily and even politically, was trying hard to modernize. Thus Japan's demand for an extension of the time limit could be easily accepted. In a few words it can be said that naval rearmament was not connected with war, whereas military rearmament had to be directly related to war.

As I showed in the previous chapter and earlier, before the Sino-Japanese and Russo-Japanese Wars, the political parties and the population at large were somewhat resistant to naval rearmament. This was because, whichever war we are talking about, the navy was the leading power compared to the army, and it knew that until its forces were up to full strength, the government would not be able to embark upon a war.

After the Russo-Japanese War, however, the situation was different. On the one hand, for the navy the possibility of going to war with the United States was close to zero, whereas for the army, which was demanding an extension of the time limit on its special rights in Manchuria and Mongolia, the possibility of entering into armed conflict with China was relatively high. Was it not because the parties and public opinion grasped this fact that they were lenient towards naval rearmament but severe in relation to rearmament of the army? The fact that in 1911 the second Saionji Cabinet (based on the *Seiyūkai*) had authorized the construction (or purchase) of three warships, but in 1912 had rejected the establishment of two extra divisions for the army, demonstrates this.

In addition, when Uehara Yūsaku, minister of war, enraged at this imbalance, independently presented his resignation to the Emperor and forced the *Seiyūkai* cabinet to resign, the political parties, the media and the urban masses came together under the slogan 'overthrow the domain clique, protect the Constitution', and a mere two months after the formation of the third Katsura cabinet, based on the army faction, forced it out of power. This was the 'Taishō political change' and I think it serves to support my hypothesis.

Concentrated fire in favour of military rearmament

Military rearmament, which was becoming the most realistic prospect from the standpoint of 'National Defence' and 'Empire', was the most unpopular in what I have previously described as a situation of mutual conflict between proliferating individual interests. This was the army that in December 1912, with the independent resignation of the Minister for War Uehara Yūsaku, forced out of office the second Saionji Cabinet, which favoured the navy, in a kind of double suicide. Tokutomi Sohō, a close confidant of Katsura Tarō, who was owner of the *Kokumin Shinbun* (national newspaper), and wrote for it as a journalist, sent the following letter, summarized here, to Terauchi Masatake, a major army figure and governor of Korea, three days after the resignation of the second Saionji Cabinet:

> After your Excellency returned to your post as Governor of Korea, the political situation in Tokyo has gone through rapid change, the so-called 'tyranny of party men' has become extreme, the collapse [of the second Saionji Cabinet] with its selfish interests is blamed on the Army, chastising men from the Army, chastising Chōshū, chastising the domain clique and so on, screaming a load of nonsense.... Moreover, chambers of commerce from Tokyo and elsewhere have disgracefully decided to oppose any increase in the number of army divisions and to support the Saionji Cabinet, this being a cover for political parties, which they follow blindly; it is completely contemptible.[1]

Let us first of all take up the point about the movement opposed to increasing the number of army divisions, introduced by Tokutomi Sohō with the words: '(t)he Chambers of Commerce from Tokyo and elsewhere.' On 4 December the Tokyo Chamber of Commerce set up a 'Committee concerning current problems', which resolved 'to act on various fronts to attempt reform of the financial administration of the Saionji Government and to reject the proposal for additional army divisions'.[2] In the midst of a situation where interest groups were proliferating after the Russo-Japanese War, the Chambers of Commerce and Industry, powerful opponents of agricultural landlords who exerted the greatest influence over Japanese politics, expressed their clear opposition to rearmament.

The army, which was the target of criticism from many sides, doubted whether the navy should be added to this as well. Ever since the previous year, when only naval rearmament had been authorized, Tanaka Giichi, who headed Military Administration in the Ministry of War, persistently appealed to the army leaders to be careful about allying themselves politically with the naval top brass. At the time of the Chinese Revolution in 1911, he sent a letter to Terauchi Masatake hinting that the 'moving force' behind suppression of the army's demand for interference in that revolution was the navy. The following is the gist of what he wrote:

> What I would like to report to you is the existence of a 'moving force' which has led the Government to commit this kind of blunder. There are those who do not rejoice at the development of our continental Empire, who only expand their own fields and fail to consider the fate of this country, and out of jealousy there are the people of one faction who do not cease from sacrificing our national destiny in order to obstruct the development of others.[3]

He uses very indirect language, but his phrase 'the people of one faction' clearly indicates central personnel of the navy. This is important as material demonstrating the conflict between the army and navy in the politics of the final year of Meiji, but we should also take note of the fact that he designates those opposing the addition of two army divisions as '(t)hose who do not rejoice at the development of our continental Empire'.

In the process of designing the Imperial Defence Policy, Tanaka criticized the navy's argument that America as a potential enemy was unrealistic. But in addition, for Tanaka the aim of the Japanese Empire was only 'development aimed at the Continent'. If they betrayed this, those opposing an increase in army divisions were people who were opposed to Japanese 'imperialism'.

The Taishō Political Crisis

The common goal of those opposed to an addition of two divisions to the army was to defend the Constitution by 'overthrowing the domain clique'. This was 'Constitution' in the broad sense to which I am referring to in this book. The movement of the city masses variously known as the 'Taishō Political Crisis' or the 'First Constitutional Defence Movement' in the first year of Taishō (1912) is a rare example of 'Empire' and 'Constitution' coming into direct conflict with each other.

Sixteen days elapsed between the resignation of the second Saionji Cabinet on 5 December 1912 (following the resignation of Uehara as minister for war), until the formation of the third Katsura cabinet on 21 December. But conflict between the army and the political parties, between the army and public opinion, and between the army and the urban masses indicated the seriousness of political unrest at the time. The inauguration of the third Katsura cabinet to some extent increased the unrest. In the opinion of the Conference of Elder Statesmen, given the relationship between Katsura and Saionji that had lasted for seven years from the end of the Russo-Japanese War, the *Seiyūkai*, which enjoyed a majority in the House of Representatives, would probably support a Katsura cabinet if one was to be formed. And if Katsura Tarō were to form a new Katsura Party based on the right wing of the *Kokumintō*, which was the leading opposition party, then other parties, fearing a dissolution, would create some distance between themselves and the popular movement, or so the elder statesmen calculated. This Katsura New Party was the forerunner of the later *Rikken Dōshikai*, leading to the *Kenseikai*, and finally to the *Rikken Minseitō*.

If these had been normal times, both the instincts of the Conference of Elder Statesmen and of Katsura Tarō would not have been wide of the mark. The *Seiyūkai* leader Hara Kei held back until the very last moment from joining the constitutional support group, until members of the party were no longer forbidden from joining this group, formed by opposition parties and journalists on newspapers and magazines. There remained room to compromise with the Katsura Cabinet. The constitutional support group itself did not consider ousting the third Katsura Cabinet by means of a movement they themselves had summoned. The group was formed on the basis of its principal premise that the third Katsura Cabinet would be dissolved during the thirtieth Diet just after its inauguration, and that general elections would be called.

Since it took a long time to organize the successor cabinet, the inauguration of the thirtieth Diet was later than usual, on 24 December. Over the New Year period the Diet is on holiday. According to practice at the time, Diet members were off work for four weeks, so that the Diet reopened on 21 January 1913. But since there were not many days to spare, Prime Minister Katsura was late with his printed copy of the budget bill. But he proposed to representatives of all the parties that the Diet should resume on 5 February. Hara Kei of the *Seiyūkai*, however, proposed that 'since the Diet should debate not only the budget, its vacation should end on 20 January', and he refused to compromise on this.[4]

This exchange between Prime Minister Katsura and Hara Kei shows that if the Diet session that began on 21 January fell into confusion, the ending of the session by 5 February, which was Katsura's initial demand, would conform to the expectations of political professionals. But for the media and the mass movement aroused by the slogans 'down with the domain clique, defend the Constitution', it reflected the tyranny of the Katsura Cabinet, which was ignoring popular opinion. The second speech meeting in defence of the Constitution, held at the Shintomiza theatre in Tsukiji on 24 January after the closure of the Diet, is said to have been the most successful meeting.

Apart from the arousal of public opinion, Prime Minister Katsura, together with the *Chūō Kurabu* (Central Club), which hitherto had supported the domain-clique as part of the *Kokumintō* (the second largest party) on 21 January, the day before the Diet reopened, formed a new party controlling 93 out of a total of 381 seats. In so doing it stole the opportunity for compromise from the leading *Seiyūkai*, which was the number one party. When the *Seiyūkai* official Noda Utarō heard about a compromise proposal from the Elder Statesman Inoue Kaoru, he commented sharply: 'Katsura has already formed a new party that is unlikely to put forward interesting proposals other than opposing our party.'[5] But in the world of political professionals it was firmly believed that when the Diet reopened on 5 February, about two weeks before the *Seiyūkai* and the *Kokumintō* together moved a motion of no-confidence in the Katsura cabinet, a kind of compromise would be worked out between the bureaucratic supporters of Katsura and the Seiyūkai, which had stuck with him for more than seven years after the Russo-Japanese War.

As I have already argued, however, the theme of a 'Constitution' after the Russo-Japanese War, at least within the cabinet and the House of Representatives, had not died down. Rallies and demonstrations of the city masses had become a key factor in the direction politics was taking.

For an opposition party fear of dissolution is a constant in any period. Even within the *Seiyūkai*, which was a party out of power despite having a parliamentary majority, there was no lack of people who wanted compromise with the Katsura cabinet in order to avoid dissolution. But Hara Kei, who succeeded Saionji Kinmochi, kept a close eye on trends in public opinion and the city masses. On the other hand, while leaving room for compromise with the Katsura Cabinet, responding to moves in public opinion and the masses, he was steering the boat step by step in the direction of a no-confidence motion against the Katsura government.

On 24 January the Constitution Defence Movement, which was little more than a large speech meeting (with about 30,000 members), created a demonstration movement in the vicinity of the Diet, coinciding with its reopening on 5 February. Hara Kei wrote in his diary on that day: 'I left the Diet at noon, outside was a noisy uproar from a mass of people.' On that day, 214 Diet members belonging to the *Seiyūkai*, excepting those absent on account of illness, came intending to cast white votes (votes in favour), and after the Diet was closed once more, Hara Kei and others spoke at the newly formed 'White Vote Association'. Hara had abandoned Katsura and stood alongside the popular masses.

From the army to the navy

I shall omit details of developments from that time until 10 February 1913, including the siege of the Diet by demonstrators, Prime Minister Katsura's resignation statement, incidents of arson against police boxes and pro-government newspapers, spreading of the movement to Ōsaka, Kōbe, Hiroshima and Kyōto, and the formation of a cabinet influenced by the navy (the first Yamamoto Gonbei Cabinet). The details of this period have already been thoroughly explored through masses of research.

There are three important points to be made from this book's standpoint of exploring modern Japanese history focusing on relations between 'Empire' and 'Constitution'.

First of all, among the constituent elements of 'Constitution' the city masses became an established factor. Already politics could no longer be managed through conflict and compromise between the bureaucratic clique and the political parties. But at the same time it became clear that street movements by the urban masses had a limited lifespan. Mass street movements following the peace treaty between Japan and Russia began with the signing of the treaty on 5 September 1905, and the conclusion of the Privy Council survey on 4 October. Similarly, the mass street movement reached its apogee on 10 February 1913. When the next cabinet was formed on 20 February, the movement ended like a wave subsiding. The issue of the journal *Nihon oyobi Nihonjin* (*Japan and the Japanese*), published at the beginning of March, expressed its disappointment and anger in the following terms: 'Why on earth has the passionate violence that occurred the other day petered out like a fire that has been quenched?'[6]

At that time, just like today, spontaneous mass demonstrations develop with a specific goal, but whether they win or lose, once the goal is no longer there they recede like the tide. Since the goal at that time was the overthrow of the third Katsura Cabinet, when Katsura resigned on 11 February, the movement quickly lost momentum. The following cabinet of Yamamoto Gonbei was also, just like the Katsura Cabinet, a military clique cabinet (in this case based on the navy), and derived from the domain-cliques, the only difference being that Satsuma replaced Chōshū. This rationale was unfavourable to the mass movement. Until the time when the Yamamoto Cabinet would provide the next target, the popular movement remained quiet.

The second point is well known. This is the retreat of the army faction and advance of the navy faction. The army goal of increasing the number of its divisions had been buried by the actions of the parties and the masses, but the goal of the navy to build more warships, derived from the second Saionji Cabinet as I have already described, had not been fulfilled, and was still the aim of the Yamamoto Cabinet. Not only that, but even though the Yamamoto Cabinet, a mere two and a half months after the Political Crisis period came to an end, had not sought the funds for naval rearmament in its 1913 budget, in its budget for 1914 it was clear to everybody that it was embarking upon a programme of naval rearmament. As I have pointed out before, since the Imperial Defence

Policy drawn up by the army with Russia and China as potential enemies, it was Yamamoto Gonbei of the navy who had been sworn in as prime minister. He had dropped China and instead inserted America, and that had forced the army to accept an expanded naval expansion programme.

The third point is the importance of the army, which had lost out to 'Constitution', and had later lost out to the navy, in the history of 'Empire' in modern Japan.

Japan before the outbreak of the Russo-Japanese War had taken control of Korea and was aiming to construct a continental empire by taking southern Manchuria. The navy had faithfully followed this aim, had defeated the Chinese Navy, and had been victorious over the Russian fleet. Even when we look back at the Taiwan expedition of 1874, the navy had already come to play a leading role in Japanese continental imperialism.

In the meantime the navy became the focus of attack from the domestic 'Constitution' movement. Before the Sino-Japanese War and before the Russo-Japanese War, the majority parties in the House of Representatives – the *Jiyūtō* and later the *Seiyūkai* – combated naval rearmament. But with the Imperial Defence Policy in 1907, when the navy designated the United States as a potential enemy, the *Seiyūkai*, whether it was in power or out of power, continuously supported naval rearmament. And so after Katsura Tarō, who was close to the army, was subjected to attack from within and outside the Diet, and then forced out of office, Yamamoto Gonbei, who came from the navy, succeeded him, and the mass movement calmed down. Not only was the army demand for extra divisions denied, but its goal of a continental empire also lost support. The establishment of the Yamamoto Gonbei government in February 1913 was symbolic of this.

The 'positive policies' of the Yamamoto Gonbei government

If in January 1914 an affair of bribery within the navy, known as the 'Siemens Incident' and involving the Yamamoto government (backed by the navy and the *Seiyūkai*), had not been detected, that government would not have been expelled from office so easily.

When the Katsura Cabinet resigned amid attacks outside the Diet by mass action, the Chōshū bureaucratic clique, the army and the Katsura New Party, for the time being, lost their influence in the political world. The mass movement outside the Diet also ran out of steam with the inauguration of the new cabinet.

Both in the House of Representatives and outside it, neither Inukai Tsuyoshi of the *Rikken Kokumintō*, nor Ozaki Yukio of the *Seiyūkai* minority faction, joined the mainstream faction of the Yamamoto Cabinet, but both for the time being regarded it with benevolent neutrality (Inukai and Ozaki were each known as 'God of the Constitution'). Now Hara Kei who replaced Saionji, becoming the third successive president of the majority *Seiyūkai*, did not simply offer cooperation from outside, but was sworn in as a cabinet minister and officially made the *Seiyūkai* the ruling party in the Yamamoto Cabinet.

Changes occurred in the seat totals of the various parties, but when the thirty-first Diet session was inaugurated in December 1913, out of 381 seats the *Seiyūkai* had 208 (55 per cent), the *Kokumintō* (a quasi-government party) and the *Chūseikai* together had 77 seats, and the *Rikken Dōshikai* (Katsura New Party) had 93 seats (just under 25 per cent). The Satsuma-based domain-clique, the navy and the majority party supported the government; the army lost political influence, and the opposition *Rikken Dōshikai* retained less than a quarter of the seats.

The Yamamoto Cabinet engaged in a wholesale reconstruction of the bureaucracy, and obtained the support of the urban Chambers of Commerce and Industry that had earlier lit the fuse of army highhandedness. Four months after the cabinet was formed, members of the Chambers of Commerce welcomed a reduction of just over 800 in the number of high officials and just over 400 lower officials. In contemporary language this was a reduction in both career and non-career officials, and the government promised a reduction in corporation tax as a result. Towards the end of July, the Tokyo Chambers of Commerce invited Prime Minister Yamamoto and other ministers to a reception, where the master of ceremonies, Nakano Buei, made the following greeting:

> Your Excellency Prime Minister Yamamoto, Honourable guests. Members of The Tokyo Chambers of Commerce express our wholehearted welcome to you. . . . Restructuring (of the bureaucracy) has been talked about by whatever government was in power, but has never been implemented, to our great regret. However, since your Excellency formed your Cabinet, your achievement of administrative and financial restructuring touches our very hearts. I would like to express my sincere appreciation of the many achievements of your cabinet ministers.[7]

Here the Tokyo Chamber of Commerce was merely praising the persistence with which the Yamamoto Cabinet was conducting a broad administrative reconstruction. But it was clear to everyone that the cabinet, headed by a serving admiral, was aiming to expand the navy. It is reasonable to suppose that this Chamber of Commerce, which about eight months earlier had openly criticized the army's plan to increase the number of its divisions, intended to approve the navy's demands for more warships.

The Yamamoto Cabinet, which enjoyed the support of the majority party and of Chambers of Commerce throughout the country, intended to support the navy's demands. In addition to the 90,000,000 yen for the three extra warships that had already been authorized by the second Saionji Cabinet before it fell from office, the Yamamoto Cabinet had passed a cabinet resolution to provide an extra 70,000,000 yen for continuing expenses as part of its second consolidation plan.

The so-called positive policies demanded by the president of the government party, the *Seiyūkai*, in his capacity as minister of the interior, were based on the premise of port construction and expansion of the railway network. The *Seiyūkai* had already reduced corporation tax by freeing up funds through administrative retrenchment. Within the Interior Ministry's budget, apart from expenditure on harbour repairs, the *Seiyūkai* and the Ministry of the Interior prevailed on the cabinet to approve the raising of 300,000,000 yen for railway expansion.

However much money was raised through administrative retrenchment so as to reduce corporation tax aimed at those working in commerce and industry, naval rearmament and expansion of the rail network could only be financed by foreign loans. In this way, although financial policy at first sight appeared unplanned, it was supported by the Finance Minister Takahashi Korekiyo, even though he came from the Bank of Japan and believed in 'positive policies' even more than did Hara Kei. Indeed, he had been active in raising foreign loans at the time of the Russo-Japanese War. As I shall argue later in modification of my argument, Takahashi, who served as minister of finance in the cabinet of Hara Kei inaugurated in 1918, totally opposed the continental empire envisaged by the army. This helps understand the relations between the Yamamoto Cabinet, with its preference for the navy over the army, and Takahashi.

The Siemens Affair

While the army and the Katsura New Party were forced to remain silent, the Yamamoto Cabinet, supported by the navy, the majority party and the Chambers of Commerce, could not find a way to take advantage of it. The 31st Diet approved 160,000,000 yen for the naval rearmament scheme, and 30,000,000 in foreign loans for railway expansion, as well as a 30 per cent reduction in corporation tax (this was rejected by the cabinet at the last stage, and the Chambers of Commerce turned against the cabinet), thinking that the Diet could reach the end of its term without problems.

On 22 January 1914, however, a naval bribery affair was reported in a Tokyo newspaper, and everything changed.

Even though they may have forgotten the details, many Japanese people will recognize the terms 'Siemens Affair'. But considering how well known the term remains, what actually happened has not been entirely established. However, this affair did not only lead to the resignation of the Yamamoto Cabinet. Nor did it only result in the breakdown of the naval rearmament plan. What upset the great naval rearmament plan, following the impasse in the plan to give the army two extra divisions, was the serious breakdown in the Imperial Defence Plan itself. That plan envisaged as potential enemies Russia, America, Germany and France (in reality just Russia, China and America). For this reason, I shall now say something about the outline of the affair.

When Richter, an employee of the German company Siemens-Schukkelt, left the Tokyo branch of the company, he took important documents with him, and sold them to Pooley of Reuters press agency for 750 yen. Among them was a document stating that when the company sold warships to the Japanese Navy: they paid a rebate (in those days it was known as commission). Pooley threatened the head of the Tokyo branch of Siemens, Hermann, and bought him off with 50,000 yen. Hermann asked the Japanese Navy to pay the 50,000 yen, but the Navy Ministry refused.

In his diary on the day after newspapers in Japan had splashed across their front pages the first account of this affair (23 January), the Vice-Minister for the Navy Takarabe Takeshi, wrote: 'In November last year, when Hermann came to visit the Navy Ministry, it was tough with him, I now feel that this response was excellent.'[8] He was not in the least perturbed by the first report about the Siemens Affair. On the contrary, he was proud of having rejected a request from the head of the Tokyo branch of the same newspaper.

It is believed that when Hermann, the head of the Tokyo branch of Siemens, asked for assistance from the Japanese Navy Ministry (it is not known whether this was before or after he had paid the *Reuters* journalist 50,000 yen), he let it be known that the Japanese Navy had received a rebate from the Siemens Company. The fact that the naval vice-minister refused this request shows that Takarabe did not believe that there was any substance in it. Another thing that needs to be taken into account is that Takarabe consulted with Matsumoto Yawara, head of the Naval Vessel Policy Department and decided to protest against Hermann's inappropriate demand to the Siemens headquarters in Germany. In his diary following his rejection of a demand from Hermann at the end of the previous year (27 November), Takarabe wrote as follows:

> I consulted with Vice-Admiral Matsumoto (Yawara), and Bureau Chief Uchida (judicial administration). I must definitely contact Siemens-Schukkelt concerning Hermann's inappropriate behaviour.[9]

As is well known, the so-called Siemens Affair became important because Matsumoto Yawara himself, who had opposed Siemens' general headquarters together with Takarabe, over this issue of Hermann, had been found to have received a bribe of 4,000,000 yen from Mitsui Bussan. The bribe had been given by the domestic headquarters of Mitsui Bussan, the warships were being purchased from the British firm Vickers, which had no connection with Siemens, and because this had happened four years before, Matsumoto concluded that it did not constitute a problem. There are many cases like this in recent corruption issues.

On 18 February 1914, however, when Matsumoto Yawara had his house searched, the game was probably up for the Yamamoto Cabinet and the navy. Matsumoto, at the end of the previous year, had been transferred from his post as head of Naval Vessel Policy Headquarters to the post of commander-in-chief of the naval station at Kure (near Hiroshima), retaining his current rank of vice-admiral, with pay not at 750 yen or 50,000 yen but at the quite different order of 400,000 yen. Even so, the Yamamoto Cabinet, supported by the majority *Seiyūkai* Party, was attempting somehow to extricate itself from these difficulties. Hara Kei, cabinet minister and de facto president of the *Seiyūkai*, maintained that the navy minister had no need to resign from his position as minister for the navy just because the house of one of his staff had been searched.

Hara Kei, de facto president of the *Seiyūkai*, which enjoyed a majority in the House of Representatives, on 10 February defeated a censure motion by a large majority. Using the power of the police, he dispersed a crowd, reported variously as amounting to 30,000 or 100,000, of those resentful at navy corruption. Two days later, on 12 February, the Yamamoto Cabinet was able to pass the budget for 1914 through the House of Representatives, and this included a total of 160,000,000 yen for naval rearmament. The scale of the popular movement was comparable to that which occurred on 10 February of the previous year, but the *Seiyūkai*, at that time supporting a no-confidence motion against the Katsura government, was now the party in power, and switched to opposing the censure

The revenge of the House of Peers

It was the House of Peers that blocked the strong-armed actions of the cabinet and the party in power when they forced the passage of a bill for major naval rearmament in the middle of a naval scandal involving the taking of bribes. By contrast with the post-war Constitution, under the Great Japan Imperial Constitution, the House of Representatives and the House of Peers had equal powers. On a budget bill, however, a decision by the House of Representatives was considered to have precedence. According to the text of the Constitution (article 65): 'The budget shall be first laid before the House of Representatives.' That is all it says, but domain-clique governments, as well as both Houses of the Diet, came to understand it as meaning that in decisions on budget bills having an important impact on people's standard of living, a decision of the House of Representatives should have precedence.

When, however, it became known that the trend of the media and mass demonstration movements was having absolutely no impact on the House of Representatives, because of the power of the ruling party enjoying a majority, public opinion drew attention to yet another article in the Meiji Constitution. Article 64 stated that 'The expenditure and revenue of the State require the consent of the Imperial Diet by means of an annual budget'. Even if the House of Representatives had passed the budget, it could not be approved by the 'Imperial Diet' if the House of Peers opposed it.

The House of Peers, consisting of titled men, including princes, marquises, counts, viscounts and barons, as well as members chosen by imperial decree following retirement, had maintained its loyalty to domain-clique governments over a long period. Members holding aristocratic titles were the successors of earlier *kuge* (court nobles) and *daimyō* (domain lords), while those chosen by imperial decree naturally originated from the bureaucracy. Among them, viscounts constituted the central hub of the House of Peers (successors of domain lords who held more than 100,000, and less than 150,000 *koku*[10] of rice), and members chosen by imperial decree originated from the Chōshū domain and were under the command of Yamagata Aritomo and Katsura Tarō. As I have shown earlier, Tokutomi Sohō in his book *Taishō seikyoku shi ron* (*A History of the Political Situation in the Taishō Era*) demonstrated that political stability after the Russo-Japanese War was based on a situation where when Katsura was prime minister, Saionji, leading the *Seiyūkai*, supported him in the House of Representatives, and when Saionji was prime minister, Katsura, in charge of the House of Peers, would assist him.

When, however, Katsura and the *Seiyūkai* clashed head-on over the issue of two extra divisions for the army, the *Seiyūkai* abandoned the Chōshū domain and joined forces with the Satsuma domain and the navy, so that their counterpart to which they swore allegiance in the House of Peers disappeared. Katsura Tarō and the army had to withdraw from the surface of the political world.

For the House of Peers, the naval bribery affair, and the fact that the *Seiyūkai* had forced the budget bill through the House of Representatives, was a supreme opportunity for revenge. Moreover, the media and the popular movement seem to have expected that the House of Peers would reject the budget bill. Den Kenjirō – leader of members appointed by Imperial Decree in the House of Peers, from the very day of the rejection of a censure motion against the cabinet, brought by the opposition parties in the House of Representatives – wrote in his diary that the people were investing their hopes in the House of Peers:

> Today, the *Dōshikai*, the *Chūseikai* and the *Kokumintō*, the three opposition parties in the lower house, have presented a censure motion, and their associates outside the Diet, having organised a national assembly in Hibiya Park, are egging them on. From morning onwards, in the vicinity of the Diet, there is a crowd amounting to several tens of thousands, a situation of savage confrontation. [Up to about the time when the censure motion was defeated by the *Seiyūkai*] the crowds outside the Diet grew still larger, around 100,000 people surrounded the House of Representatives, and there was nowhere to stand. Diet members in the opposition parties gradually left the scene, happily accepting cheers from the crowd. But Ministers and *Seiyūkai* members were unable to leave by the chamber door. Members of our House of Peers, holding up a large bamboo placard advertising our House in large letters, went forward, and safely found their way home.[11]

The very fact that a member of the House of Peers on the scene at the time should have written in his diary on 10 February about the interactions between the cabinet, the party in power, the parties out of power and the people outside the Diet concerning the motion to censure the cabinet gives a sense of on-the-spot immediacy. Despite the fact that the censure motion was rejected in the House of Representatives, the members of the opposition party and the masses outside the Diet do not appear to have been downcast by this experience. So despite the fact that cabinet members and members of the *Seiyūkai*, surrounded by the crowds, were unable to leave the Diet building, Den Kenjirō of the House of Peers, and others, protected by a bamboo placard as he described, were able to open a way out as a group, just like members of opposition parties.

The collapse of both the navy cabinet and the *Seiyūkai*

This trend became even more striking when the *Seiyūkai* asked for figures in the House of Representatives, and approved the 1914 budget, of which 160,000,000 yen were for continuing military expenditures (90,000,000 yen already approved by the opposition parties, and 70,000,000 yen to which the opposition parties were opposed). The right of the House of Peers to debate the budget, mentioned earlier, was something in which the media and the popular movement were beginning clearly to place expectations. About two weeks after the budget bill had been sent from the House of Representatives to the House of Peers, the secretariat of the group of viscounts that held the real authority in the House of Peers, and the group of members appointed by Imperial Decree (the *Kenkyūkai* [research group] and *Saiwai* [happiness] *Club*), decided to oppose in the House of Peers the new sum of 70,000,000 yen. In his diary for that day (28 February), Den Kenjirō wrote as follows:

> The situation regarding the Navy has suddenly become infuriating, it has resulted in serious unrest in Tokyo, it has caused confusion in the lower house, each newspaper company has become a great alliance, people's feelings are perturbed and public opinion is becoming far too explosive. We can only rack our brains, respect the positions of the upper house whatever they may be, and just hope.[12]

The popular movement, the media and the House of Peers, acting as one, stood opposed to the Yamamoto Cabinet and the House of Peers. So the plenary session of the House of Peers on 13 March, by a wide margin of 240 versus 44, cut 70,000,000 yen earmarked for supplementary naval construction expenditure from the budget that had been approved by the House of Representatives, and with that budget deliberations ended. A bill identical to that presented in the House of Representatives by the three opposition parties – the *Dōshikai*, the *Kokumintō* and the *Chūseikai* – became a decision of the House of Peers.

Under the present Constitution, in circumstances where the House of Representatives and the House of Councillors arrive at different decisions over the budget, a joint committee of both houses may be held, but if opinions still remain divided, the decision of the House of Representatives becomes the decision of the Diet.

In the case of general bills, they can be resubmitted by a two-thirds majority (when rejected by the House of Councillors), but this is not necessary in the case of the budget. Under the Meiji Constitution, however, with no precedence of one house over the other, the budget-making power of either house was equal to that of the other. As with the present Constitution, when the two houses made conflicting decisions, a committee of both houses was held, but a plenary session of each house then had to be consulted over the decision.

Prime Minister Yamamoto and people connected with the navy requested that the House of Representatives would compromise, accepting a reduction of 70 million yen, and requested at a committee of both Houses of the Diet that the remaining 90 million yen for naval expansion should be protected. Hara Kei, however, representing the *Seiyūkai*, resolved that, even if the budget were not passed, the custom of giving priority to decisions of the House of Representatives should be maintained.

A committee of both houses, having an equal number of members from each of the two houses, perhaps because of the custom of prioritizing decisions from the House of Representatives, came to appoint a chairman from the House of Peers. On the House of Peers side, there was one member less than on the side of the House of Representatives. Here if it had adhered to the decision of both houses, the committee of both houses would have resolved in favour of the House of Representatives decision, including 70,000,000 yen of new spending for naval rearmament, but instead, the decision of the committee of both houses was submitted to a plenary session of each house.

As expected, this is what happened. The plenary session of the House of Representatives once again accepted the 160,000,000 yen resolution, but the plenary session of the House of Peers on 23 March rejected the decision of the committee of both houses. Because the budget of the previous year was put into operation, the budget for 1914 itself became null and void. Because the budget of the previous year was revived (Constitution, article 71), the 160,000,000 yen for naval rearmament, including the 90,000,000 for three new warships, which had already been decided at cabinet level during the second Saionji Cabinet, sank into oblivion. On 24 March, the Yamamoto Cabinet resigned.

8

The twenty-one demands to China
'Constitution' domestically, 'Empire' externally

The rise of Yoshino Sakuzō

The point of reference throughout this book is the idea that when 'Constitution' was strong, 'Empire' was restrained, and when 'Empire' was strong, 'Constitution' ran out of breath. The idea of 'Constitution domestically, Empire externally', meaning that both of them coexisted simultaneously, is however mistaken as a way of understanding Japanese modern history. But during the second cabinet of Ōkuma Shigenobu (April 1914–October 1916), which came to office following the ending of the Taishō Political Crisis, the contrast between the domestic and the external situation did fit this model exceptionally.

This cabinet, which absorbed the results of the Taishō Political Crisis, institutionalized 'Constitution'. In so far as the controlling regime after the Russo-Japanese War was a cooperative enterprise between the military clique, the bureaucratic clique and the *Seiyūkai* as the eternal ruling party, the Siemens Affair, in which the masses targeted the *Seiyūkai*, may be regarded as the culmination of the Taishō Political Crisis.

The second Ōkuma Cabinet was a kind of 'non-*Seiyūkai*' Cabinet consisting of what may be called a 'government party', or a 'quasi-government party', including the *Rikken Dōshikai* of Katō Takaaki, the *Rikken Kokumintō* of Inukai Tsuyoshi, and the *Chūseikai* of Ozaki Yukio. The *Seiyūkai*, for the first time since its foundation, was forced into the position of a party in the political wilderness. Ever since the Imperial Edict establishing a Constitutional Regime, issued in 1875, which had meant combining confrontation with cooperation between the domain-clique and the parties, what seems now to have arrived was a system of two major parties competing for power between them.

In the election law at the time, however, a large majority of the 1,500,000 electors were rural landlords, and since the 'three anti-*Seiyūkai* factions' forming the government party behind the Ōkuma Cabinet engaged in continual combat with the *Seiyūkai*, there was no alternative but to expand the electoral roll and pick up votes from the city commercial and industrial classes, as well as the votes of ordinary people. The man who presented this idea most clearly was Professor Yoshino Sakuzō of Tokyo Imperial University, who had recently returned from Europe and America. Just after the formation of the second Ōkuma Cabinet, the journal *Taiyō* (*Sun*) published an article by Yoshino, titled 'The collapse of the Yamamoto Cabinet and the establishment of the Ōkuma Cabinet'. This was a rare example of an analysis of the unfolding drama of a change of government from the viewpoint of a political scientist with a long-term perspective.

Yoshino presented the differences between the party politics he himself had witnessed in Western Europe between 1910 and 1913, and party politics in Japan.

> For a long time Japanese political parties have only been able to expand their party base once they have obtained power, but this is just the opposite of parties in the advanced countries of Western Europe. In their case, they can only come to power once they have developed their party strength among the people. . . . Moreover, when we survey the parties in our country, even if you have a majority in the Diet, it is still very difficult to come to power or to hope to maintain power. And so, to lose power means that party strength quickly atrophies. [Therefore], however many insults are thrown in their direction, such as 'idiot' or 'fool', they will try not to be alienated from power.

For a long time I have protested against the argument that the West is fine but Japan is no good, and I have insisted that democracy made progress in pre-war Japan. When, however, one examines recent Japanese politics, perhaps Yoshino Sakuzō was right. Unless when party A is in power but makes a mess of things, party B is ready to assume power, and when party B is not effective in government, party A is able to prepare to return to power – a system based on two major parties will not function. If when a party loses office, its 'party strength quickly atrophies', but however many insults it receives, it will 'try not to be alienated from power', and party politics will not progress.

The argument about introducing universal suffrage

From this perspective, Yoshino first of all called for the strengthening of solidarity between the three 'non-*Seiyūkai*' factions. In order to reject constant single-party dominance by the *Seiyūkai*, it was essential to maintain the solidarity of the opposing forces. Of course this should develop into a single party, but he explained that for the time being what was needed was the strengthening of solidarity among the three factions.

Yoshino's second point was the introduction of universal suffrage. What should be noted here is that Yoshino was not putting this forward on the basis of democratic principles, but because of the need for the three anti-*Seiyūkai* factions to broaden their base of support. Only by fortifying the solidarity of the 'three anti-*Seiyūkai* factions', could they become a party able to contest the supremacy of the *Seiyūkai*. What was needed was to broaden the base of party support. Moreover, this base of support must become semi-permanent. In summary, Yoshino was insisting that unless the 'three anti-*Seiyūkai* factions' were able to create their own independent base of support (*jiban*), they would not create a force able to contest the hegemony of the *Seiyūkai*.

At that time the total number of voters was about 1,500,000, the majority of whom constituted the *jiban* (base of support) of the *Seiyūkai*. A new party (based on the three non-*Seiyūkai* factions), able to contest the *Seiyūkai*, would have to create its own base of support outside these 1,500,000 electors. If universal suffrage were introduced, the number of electors would increase to over 12,000,000. Yoshino's universal suffrage argument at that time (March 1914) was that in that way a new party would be able to build a base of support.

Two years and five months later, in October 1916, although there were some comings and goings in the meantime, the three non-*Seiyūkai* factions formed a new party called the *Kenseikai*, with Katō Takaaki as its president. Under a cabinet having Katō as prime minister (1924–5), a system of universal male suffrage was established. This was eleven years after Yoshino's treatise, cited earlier, was published. In order to appreciate his foresight, I will quote in his own words the introduction to universal suffrage that Yoshino published in May 1914:

> Secondly, at this time of great excitement, I wish this force to become even stronger. The three factions together are insufficient to match the *Seiyūkai* on its own, and if party cabinets are going to continue, they are helpless. Of course, if in present circumstances and with their strength as at present the Diet were to be dissolved, it is possible that inroads could be made into the strength of the *Seiyūkai*. Nevertheless, I cannot necessarily be confident that the majority position of the *Seiyūkai* could be overturned. . . . On the basis of this I would like to address the new party and warn that it is essential to cultivate the ground for a new base of support (*jiban*) different from that of the *Seiyūkai*. Putting it a different way, I should warn that, in striving for universal suffrage, which is the desire of most of the people, you should cultivate the position among the

people that the right to vote must be won. Fighting for the same base of support as the *Seiyūkai* with the electoral law as it is would make it most problematic to overtake the *Seiyūkai*.¹

Precisely in its calling for the introduction of universal suffrage, Yoshino's article was written in a fashion that we can easily understand today. Apart from some minor linguistic updating, I have kept it as it was in the original.

The content of Yoshino's argument in this straightforward piece is easy for us to understand today. In order to compete against a majority party, what you need is a base of support (*jiban*). Temporary popularity is no use. In this presentation by Yoshino, who was asserting the need for universal suffrage from the standpoint of a base of support, there is much that rings true for us today. For us today there is no way to broaden further the electorate, but when we examine the low rates of voter turnout, it goes without saying that we may ask where the opposition parties might construct a new *jiban*.

Key points of 'Constitution'

As is evident from Yoshino's contemporary-sounding analysis, however high the level of expectation might have been, the second Ōkuma Cabinet was the most promising in relation to 'Constitution' of any government over the forty and more years since the Meiji Restoration.

This book has taken as the starting point of 'Constitution' the Imperial Edict on the establishment of a constitutional political system in April 1875, but at that time the timetable for its implementation was not made clear, and there was merely a promise in the name of the Emperor that it would gradually evolve towards a constitutional system. The next stage, in the form of the 'Imperial Edict on the establishment of a Diet' merely interpreted 'gradually' as implementation in 1890, once again in the name of the Emperor. In 1890 the Diet opened its doors on time according to that promise, but the cabinet did not include a single member of a political party, and the cabinet was 'transcendental', that is to say, consisting of members outside the Diet. The electorate was no more than about 500,000.

And then in 1914, twenty years later, the 'three non-*Seiyūkai* factions' came to power, and when universal male suffrage was introduced (in 1925), the size of the electorate increased eight times from about 1,500,000 to 12,000,000, and the political world was suddenly democratized.

From 'Constitution' to 'Empire'

The second Ōkuma Cabinet, however, did not only consist of democrats like Yoshino Sakuzō. The army also – whose demand for extra divisions was rejected twice by the *Seiyūkai*, once under the second Saionji Cabinet and once under the Yamamoto Cabinet – found their expectations raised with the *Seiyūkai* not included in this cabinet. The two extra army divisions were to reinforce Japanese rights in southern Manchuria, and as I have already explained, the background to this lay in the 1923 crisis. In other words, those supporting 'Empire' placed strong hopes in the Ōkuma Cabinet.

The rapprochement of the army with the Ōkuma Cabinet had already begun from the most successful period of the Yamamoto Cabinet; Tanaka Giichi's name has already been mentioned several times (major-general, head of the second infantry brigade). In a letter he sent in July 1913 to Terauchi Masatake, who followed Yamagata Aritomo as head of the armed forces, he argued broadly as follows:

> Today the extreme violence of the *Seiyūkai* is of course unacceptable. [If Prince Katsura Tarō were to die], everyone would agree that of course a split in the new party Katsura founded must be prevented, and that on the contrary its development must be promoted more intensively (so long as the party still exists) Therefore, I think that as a convenient means for a short time, Ōkuma should be made President of the new party, and the non-*Seiyūkai* factions should take generous attitudes of mutual compromise, so that as in the former *Daidō danketsu* movement, reception centres should be set up and the *Kokumintō* should be absorbed.[2]

Inukai Tsuyoshi of the *Kokumintō* and Ozaki Yukio of the *Chūseikai* criticised both the *Seiyūkai* and also the Katsura New Party. When Ōkuma Shigenobu had founded the *Rikken Kaishintō* 31 years earlier (1882), they had hastened to be under his wing, and remained in a master-pupil relationship with him. A letter from Tanaka said that the Army should propel Ōkuma into the presidency of the new party (*Rikken Dōshikai*), and that through this they should place the three non-*Seiyūkai* factions under his patronage. On this point it may be said that Tanaka Giichi of the Army was the forerunner of Yoshino's proposal to unify the three non-*Seiyūkai* factions.

Nevertheless, in contrast to Yoshino's linking of his proposal for two large parties with his support for universal suffrage, for Tanaka it was all of a piece with his advocacy of two extra army divisions. And his motive for having two more divisions stationed in Korea was to strengthen Japanese rights and privileges in southern Manchuria. If Yoshino's advocacy of two large parties was directed towards the development of 'Constitution', the fact that the army was pressing for the same thing was aimed at the development of 'Empire'.

The First World War and the twenty-one demands to China

When European nations split between the Triple Entente of Russia, France and Great Britain on the one hand, and the Triple Alliance between Germany, Austria-Hungary and Italy on the other hand (though Italy later became neutral), and plunged into the world war (July–August 1914), the Ōkuma Cabinet changed direction from 'Constitution' towards 'Empire'. There is no doubt at all that the twenty-one demands to China were related to this.

What in fact had been concluded were the treaty of four articles concerning Shandong Province, and the nine-article treaty on southern Manchuria and the eastern part of Inner Mongolia, thus totalling thirteen articles, and apart from these the exchange of official documents between the Japanese consul in China and the head of the Chinese Foreign Ministry. But on 18 January the demands of the Japanese government transmitted to the Chinese government did in fact constitute the twenty-one demands.

It was natural that the Chinese side should have continued to call this treaty by its initial title of 'Twenty-one Demands'. This was in order to insist that China had been forced by Japan to swallow the twenty-one rights and interests, as well as interference in China's domestic affairs. But on the Japanese side as well, the treaty was called 'the Twenty-one Demands'. And in Japan at that time, as we have seen, Yoshino Sakuzō, the most radical constitutional advocate, gave a favourable reaction to the proposal that the demands should be divided up into twenty-one items. In the June 1915 issue of *Chūō Kōron*, he argued in the following way:

> The Chinese think that the more articles there are in a treaty, the greater the burdens they will have to bear, and the fact is that they do not welcome this. But if you just decide only the main principles, that will create much harm later on. Even if it is troublesome at first, once you scrutinise the articles one by one, they become easy enough to understand, and if you adopt this approach, in the end it is advantageous.[3]

To supplement this point, Yoshino, who nine years before was home tutor to the son of the prominent figure Yuan Shih-Kai, wrote as follows about his personal experiences during his stay in China:

My own experience may be useful in understanding this. Having accepted an invitation from Mr. Yuan Shih-Kai, I have come to Tientsin and entered into a contract of employment. In detail, this means that I must be responsible for good mutual relations between gentlemen. I have confined myself to setting out the main points in a document, but for reasons that I don't understand this has led to inconvenience and lack of benefit. It is acceptable not to write a document, but if we do, I have a deep sense that everything should be decided in the finest detail.[4]

It is hardly absurd to place in the same context the Chinese people in Yoshino's account of a personal failure and their attitudes to the twenty-one demands. I think that in this piece of writing he had to go into the fine details of the Chinese with whom he was interacting. The title of this article was 'A Criticism of Foreign Policy towards China', but his criticism did not include the twenty-one demands themselves.

Disdain for China, disdain for America

The point is often forgotten that the principal issue with the twenty-one demands was that the Japanese government had forgotten that China was a 'potential enemy' in the 'Imperial Defence Policy' immediately after the Russo-Japanese War. At that time, in order to defend the rights in southern Manchuria ceded to Japan by Russia after the time limit on returning those rights in 1923, China had been designated as a 'potential enemy' second only to Russia. If this was the case, then seven demands would have been sufficient, not twenty-one. In other words, this was a second version, consisting of seven demands, starting with article 1: 'The two contracting parties promise to extend to 99 years the lease on Lushun (Ryōjun, Port Arthur) and Dalian (Dairen), as well as on the South Manchurian Railway and the Anpô Railway.' In truth, if it had just been version 2, article 1, this would have been sufficient to clear the 1923 issue, and for Japan it would have been quite enough.

Nevertheless, Akashi Motojirō, who backed the Ōkuma cabinet, replaced Tanaka Giichi as deputy-chief of the general staff, and he did not regard China as a 'potential enemy'. Rather, after the war broke out, he maintained that the great powers of Europe and America now lacked sufficient power to interfere in relations between Japan and China.

Akashi understood, not only the lease extension to rights in Manchuria and Mongolia but also that as an additional participant in the First World War, Japan had stolen German rights to Shandong Province. The Chinese government and people were fiercely opposed to the twenty-one demands, including no. 15, the highly unpopular article 5. On 3 February 1915, in a letter to the governor of Korea, Terauchi Masatake, Akashi wrote that the position of the Chinese media was 'moving in a radical direction', and that in the future it was likely to become even more radical. Akashi also reported that the Chinese side had to some extent managed to extract itself from a difficult situation, and intended 'to wait until peace returned to Europe before moving to counterattack'.[5]

Nevertheless, the grounds for transmitting to the army top brass his resolution to press hard for the twenty-one demands were to be found in the attitudes of the European great powers. And the Foreign Ministry agreed with Akashi's judgement. In his letter Akashi argued as follows:

> Not only does Russia not differ on this, but rather it exhibits a friendly attitude concerning this issue, . . . moreover it is the view of the Foreign Ministry that Great Britain has no reason to oppose it, and most people agree that there is not much to be said about the United States.

While Japanese rights and privileges in southern Manchuria were strengthened, those of Russia in northern Manchuria were indirectly stabilized. In Great Britain, which had special rights in a key part of China, there was no reason to oppose the strengthening of Japanese rights in Manchuria. Before the First World War the United States was not a major player in international politics and did not enjoy anything in China that could be called special rights. If we take as our premise 'imperialist foreign policy' before the First World War, what the vice-chief of the general staff, Akashi, said about it was not without reason.

However, after the First World War broke out, the existing world order was seriously destabilized. In February 1915, when this letter was written, it would have been impossible to predict the Russian Revolution of October 1917. It would also have been beyond the bounds of possibility to forecast specifically the fourteen peace principles of Woodrow Wilson, who in January 1918 proclaimed national self-determination.

Nevertheless, even after the war ended, Japanese rights in Manchuria and Mongolia were protected by the Anglo-British Alliance and by the Japan–Russian entente, so that if agreement were reached between the two countries, and if there were no problems in further expanding the special rights, what further use would there be for the idea that China was a potential enemy? Moreover, while Great Britain and Russia on the one side and Germany on the other were in the middle of an all-out war, it would not need great foresight to predict that this newly minted great power, the United States of America would have more than enough to say.

Again, if we consider the future of relations between Japan and China, there was great antipathy to the twenty-one demands on the part of the Chinese people. The figure of Akashi, insisting that 'this situation will only become exacerbated' and that without any possibility of contradiction force should be used, is surely an example of the traditional 'disdain for China' shown repeatedly in this book. When he was army minister, when he was chief of the general staff, and when he was an elder statesman, Yamagata Aritomo consistently insisted that China was strong and ought not to be disparaged. In this he may be seen as an exception to the rule.

The bill for disparaging America and the bill for holding China in low esteem was something Japan had to pay after the end of the First World War.

A strange political party – split between peace and democracy

Japanese political parties – from the Meiji period until the movement to defend the Constitution in the early Taishō period – did not actively pursue 'Empire', but could not be said to have deliberately opposed it. The Ōkuma Cabinet, however, based on the three non-*Seiyūkai* parties (of which Yoshino Sakuzō expected so much), in foreign policy imposed the twenty-one demands on China, and in domestic policy authorized an increase of two divisions for the army. This last was a proposal that had been a target of attack by the Constitution Defence Movement.

As I have already noted, the origin of the Constitution Defence Movement lay in the army's demands for two additional divisions, and it forced the resignation of the *Seiyūkai* Cabinet. When the budget, including provision for additional divisions, was presented, the outbreak of the First World War resulted in public opinion moving in favour of rearmament, but the *Seiyūkai* could not approve it. The *Seiyūkai* had gone into opposition, but when that party, which had enjoyed a majority up to the presentation of the budget, opposed it, the budget was not rejected, but rather the House was dissolved. For the first time since it was founded in 1900, the *Seiyūkai* was having to fight a general election having gone into opposition (December 1914 dissolution; March 1915 general elections).

The election results showed that the *Seiyūkai*, which had 184 seats at dissolution (when the budget bill failed to pass, 18 members defected from the party), was reduced to a 104-seat total, so that the party had suddenly lost 80 seats. Hara Kei, who was *Seiyūkai*'s president, confided in his diary on 26 March after learning the election results: 'Our party majority lasting over ten years has turned into a great defeat.'

From this book's perspective, what is important is that between dissolution of the Diet on 25 December and general elections on 25 March, the twenty-one demands had been forced on China. Article 13 of the Meiji Constitution stated: 'The Emperor declares war, makes peace and concludes treaties.' Thus, the foreign policy powers of declaring war, making peace and concluding treaties were not accorded to the Diet, and if the Japanese people had opposed the twenty-one demands, the three parties backing the Ōkuma Cabinet (the *Dōshikai*, the Independent Group and the *Chūseikai*) would probably not have won 244 seats out of 381. The non-*Seiyūkai* Party that coalesced into the *Kenseikai* in October 1916, of which Katō Takaaki was later president, attracted the votes of 680,000 electors (out of 1,420,000 valid votes), and supported the twenty-one demands to China in foreign policy, and two additional divisions for the army in domestic policy. One half of the electorate supported a strange political party that proposed 'Constitution' and 'Empire' both together.

This strange non-*Seiyūkai* Party, even after it joined up with the *Kenseikai* in October 1916, supported the twenty-one demands in foreign policy, and continued to advocate the introduction of universal suffrage in domestic policy. The *Kenseikai* abandoned 'Empire externally' when a constitutional defence cabinet was formed in June 1924. This was five and a half years after the end of the First World War.

As I shall set out in Part III, the world order following the First World War, represented by the nine-nation Washington Treaty (February 1922) that proclaimed the maintenance of Chinese sovereignty and territory, constituted a negation of 'Empire'. At the same time it was a period when, within many countries, the scope of democracy was expanding, while socialism and social democracy were competing in the projection of glamour.

While this was happening, Japan alone was unable to deny 'Empire', and did not even manage to create a system of universal suffrage, which was the minimum standard for democracy after the Great War. The *Seiyūkai*, which before the war was over, continued to flourish in the government, embraced the new world order that rejected 'Imperialism', but also resisted the introduction of universal suffrage into domestic Japanese politics. On the other hand, the *Kenseikai*, which had become a party out of power, in this post-war world, continued to support the twenty-one demands, whereas in domestic politics it advocated the introduction of universal suffrage (we are talking of suffrage confined to males). Japanese politics from after the First World War, in a situation where 'peace' and 'democracy' were split apart, was unable to overcome such distortions, and was approaching the tragic dénouement that I shall investigate in Part III.

Part III

The End of 'Constitution' and 'Empire'

1918–37

Year	Event
1918	Siberian expedition. Hara Cabinet formed.
1919	1 March independence movement in Korea. 4 April movement in China. Versailles Treaty. Electoral reform (vote given to those paying more than 3 yen in tax).
1920	League of Nations founded; Japan joins. Post-war financial panic begins. Major demonstrations in Tokyo for universal suffrage. Fourteenth general election (*Seiyūkai* wins absolute majority).
1921	Hara Kei shot dead at Tokyo station. At Washington Conference (to 1922) four-power treaty signed.
1922	Nine-power Treaty – Naval Disarmament Treaty. Shandong Peninsula leasing rights returned to China (Shandong outstanding issues Treaty).
1924	*Seiyūkai* splits. *Seiyūhontō* founded (Tokonami Tokujirō). Second Constitution Defence Movement. Three faction Constitution Defence Cabinet (*Kenseikai, Seiyūkai, Kakushin Club*) formed. Progress of Shidehara diplomacy (conciliation diplomacy).
1925	Japan–Soviet Basic Treaty. Peace Preservation Law. Universal Suffrage Law.
1926	Chiang Kai-shek begins northern expedition (to 1928).
1927	Financial panic. Tanaka Giichi *Seiyūkai* Cabinet formed. (Tanaka diplomacy). Eastern Conference. Kwantung Army sets out for Shandong (to 1928). *Kenseikai* merges with *Seiyūhontō*, forms *Rikken Minseitō*.
1928	General elections under universal suffrage. 3/15 Incident. Sainan Incident. Chiang Tso-Lin assassinated. Paris No-War Treaty.
1929	World Depression. Hamaguchi Osachi *Minseitō* Cabinet formed.
1930	Second general elections under universal suffrage (*Minseitō* wins majority). London Naval Disarmament Treaty.
1931	Manchurian Incident takes place (Liutiaokou Incident).

(*Continued*)

Year	Event
1932	Shanghai Incident. League of Nations Lytton Commission of Enquiry. Eighteenth general elections (Minority party in power wins clear majority). Establishment of the State of Manchukuo. 5-15 Incident (Inukai Tsuyoshi assassinated). Saitō Minoru (national unity cabinet). Social Masses Party formed. Japan-Manchukuo Protocol signed.
1933	Japan leaves League of Nations. Tanggu (Tankū) agreement to cease hostilities between China and Japan. Nazi regime established in Germany.
1934	Manchukuo Imperial regime established. Okada Keisuke Cabinet inaugurated.
1935	Emperor organ theory of Minobe Tatsukichi questioned. Clarification statement of the National Polity (*kokutai*). Nagata Tetsuzan, head of the Army Military Affairs Bureau, stabbed to death.
1936	Nineteenth general elections (*Minseitō* overwhelming victory, *Seiyūkai* routed. *Shakai Taishūtō* makes big gains). 2-26 Incident (Saitō Makoto, Takahashi Korekiyo and others assassinated). Hirota Kôki Cabinet inaugurated. Japan–Germany Defence Pact. Washington and London treaties become void.
1937	Seppuku controversy. Ugaki Kazushige Cabinet aborted. Hayashi Senjūrō Cabinet inaugurated. Twentieth general elections (*Minseitō-Seiyūkai* conflict; *Shakai Taishūtō* makes big gains). First Konoe Fumimaro Cabinet inaugurated. Japan–China War begins (Marco Polo Bridge Incident). Axis Pact between Japan, Germany and Italy. Imperial headquarters set up.

Introduction

Japan between the two wars

The focus of Part III is the period of about twenty years between the two world wars. I shall investigate relations between 'Empire' and 'Constitution' in Japan over that period. I focus attention on the inter-war period because in the Second World War, Japan as a major player forgot about 'Constitution' and expended all its efforts on 'Empire', so that we enter a period in which this book's central theme no longer applied.

This period of a little over twenty years, known as 'Shōwa history', together with the history that immediately preceded it, is relatively well known. But in fact the key focus of research on this period has been placed on the development of 'Empire'. Research on 'Constitution' has centred on 'Taishō Democracy', whereas in so-called Shōwa history, the main emphasis has been on 'military fascism'.

In contrast to the general impression that in the Taishō period (1912–26) it was all 'Constitution' and in the Shōwa period (from 1926) it was all 'Empire', in Part III, I shall take the Taishō and Shōwa periods, and just as in Parts I and II, I shall examine the mutual relations between 'Empire' and 'Constitution'.

Departing, however, from Parts I and II, in Chapter 9 of Part III, I shall give an overview of relations between an 'Empire' and a 'Constitution' over the period as a whole, and in Chapter 10 I shall present a certain amount of detailed analysis of certain examples underpinning this 'overview'. I will refrain from explaining this narrative method in this Introduction, and will now launch directly into the 'general perspective'.

9
What happened between the two world wars?

A new world order

After the ending of the First World War in November 1918, the world order changed greatly. If we consider this in relation to Japan, the Russian Empire, which had become an important element in decision-making on China policy, had collapsed after the revolution, and the United States, which had hardly been taken seriously by Japan, replaced Great Britain as the world's hegemonic power. America, which promoted the self-determination of peoples, and proclaimed its respect for the rights and independence of China, now being placed at the centre of the world order, breathed new life into the movement to restore rights within China.

Within this global change, Japan was constrained to return to China the rights that it had managed to expand during the Great War, with the exception of its rights over Manchuria and Mongolia. As a result of the Washington Conference in 1921 and 1922, Japan promised to return to China the former German rights in Shandong Province, which had been one of the twenty-one demands (the treaty to resolve the outstanding issues relating to Shandong). Japan after the Great War was urged to retreat and constrain development of the 'Empire'.

On the other hand, as a result of the success of the Russian Revolution and of mass mobilization during the Second World War, Japan had to take account not only of 'freedom' but also of 'equality'. The expansion of the Labour Party in the victorious Great Britain, and the establishment of the Weimar Republic in the defeated Germany, symbolized the global trend. From the perspective of this book that regards the modern history of Japan on the axis of relations between 'Empire' and 'Constitution', Japan after the war was approaching a period of conspicuous retreat from 'Empire' and of advance for 'Constitution'.

The great conversion of the *Seiyūkai*

Among these two things, the tendency for 'Empire' to retreat began to show signs of a reversal around 1927–8. While in China demands for the rights in Manchuria and Mongolia to be returned were strengthening, some people in Japan were jettisoning the defensive position of protecting Japanese rights in Manchuria and Mongolia, and elements were arising that wanted to convert Manchuria and Mongolia into permanent possessions of Japan. Moreover, from a quite different direction, forces able to approve the demand to win back its rights over Manchuria and Mongolia from China appeared within the 'Constitution' side. The *Seiyūkai*, which ever since its foundation in 1900 had consistently opposed 'Empire', went through a great conversion.

It would be exaggerated to say that the *Seiyūkai* supported the position advanced by some within the army that Manchuria and Mongolia should be Japanese sovereign territory. But after Tanaka Giichi became president of the *Seiyūkai* in 1925, the party showed nostalgia for the Empire of Japan at the time of the twenty-one demands, and took as their model the Japanese Empire at the time of the Anglo-Japanese Alliance. Tanaka's *Seiyūkai* inherited the policy towards Britain and Europe of the *Kenseikai* during the Katō Takaaki period. The middle ranks of the army that directed their attention to Manchuria and Mongolia wanted to build a 'New Empire', whereas the *Seiyūkai* from Tanaka's time wanted to preserve the 'Old Empire'.

The failure of Shidehara diplomacy – the Manchurian Incident

In the midst of all this, a new period in foreign policy arrived, revising the policy of accommodating the United States, and changing the pattern of Japan–China relations that the *Seiyūkai* had conducted in the era of Hara Kei. Those who inherited these changes were the newly arrived leaders of the *Kenseikai*, replacing Katō Takaaki, namely Hamaguchi Osachi, Shidehara Kijūrō and Wakatsuki Reijirō.

One of the global trends following the Great War, democracy, was quickly taken on board by the *Kenseikai*. By contrast with the *Seiyūkai* under Hara Kei, when the electorate totalled a mere 3,000,000, the *Kenseikai* led by Katō Takaaki in 1925 brought in universal suffrage, even though the right to vote was confined to males over the age of twenty-five.

Since a large majority of men over twenty-five, given the harsh realities of their lives, had probably given up on the idealism of their youth, this age restriction no doubt exercised a particularly important influence. Even so, however, the three million electors of the Hara Kei Cabinet period had suddenly quadrupled to twelve million. Following an expression I have used earlier in this book, the *Kenseikai* following the Great War represented the principle of 'Constitution domestically'.

When this party, the *Kenseikai,* abandoning 'Empire externally', launched 'Shidehara diplomacy', the fact was that a party had arisen, even in pre-war Japan, that came close to espousing the doctrine of 'peace and democracy'. Between 1929 and 1931, while the successor of the *Kenseikai*, now known as the *Rikken Minseitō* (henceforth *Minseitō*), held power, this was the high point of 'peace and democracy'.

At this point, however, the *Minseitō* Cabinet was subjected to attack from the *Seiyūkai*, constituting the 'old Empire faction', and also from the army, which was the 'new Empire faction'. In 1930 it was attacked by the opposition *Seiyūkai* Party over its signature of the London Naval Disarmament Treaty, and in 1931 over its handling of the Manchurian (Liutiaokou) Incident (the unauthorized takeover of Manchuria in September 1931 by army elements, leading to its rebirth as the Japanese-controlled state of Manchukuo); it suffered attacks from the Kwantung Army and the right wing of the army in Japan. Strictly speaking, the reason for the fall of the *Minseitō* Cabinet led by Wakatsuki Reijirō was disunity within the cabinet concerning the formation of a coalition cabinet with the *Seiyūkai*, to succeed the single-party *Minseitō* Cabinet, but seen from a longer-term perspective, it was the result of the army's 'new Empire faction' and the 'old Empire faction' of the *Seiyūkai* working together to intensify their attacks, with the Manchurian Incident as their opportunity. These two 'Empire' factions engineered the destruction of the *Minseitō* Cabinet which had been based on the principles of peace and democracy. What replaced it was the *Seiyūkai* Cabinet of Inukai Tsuyoshi.

In fact the two 'Empire' factions were not an insuperable obstacle. The 5-15 Incident (15 May 1932), in which a young naval officer (who must have been a member of the 'new Empire faction') shot Prime Minister Inukai Tsuyoshi of the *Seiyūkai* Cabinet's 'old Empire faction', indicates the incompleteness of this alliance.

The young army officers who were later to perpetrate the 2-26 Incident (26 February 1936), and the *Kantōgun*, which had already carried out the Manchurian Incident, were supporting the Inukai Cabinet that had appointed Araki Sadao as minister for war, who belonged to the army's right-wing faction.

The fact that the young naval officers and others had shot Inukai was, even for them, beyond imagination. The fact is that, as a result, the plot to seize power drawn up by the army right wing was thwarted.

The formal recognition of Manchukuo

The extension of 'Empire' as the principle of foreign policy, over about eight months between the end of the *Minseitō* Cabinet and the collapse of the *Seiyūkai* Cabinet headed by Inukai, took place in a fashion that was irreversible. Under the Inukai Cabinet that replaced the *Minseitō* Cabinet of Wakatsuki Reijirō, which had resisted any further extension of the Liutiaokou Incident of 18 September 1931, preparatory steps for formal recognition of Manchukuo in September 1932 were put firmly in place.

Official recognition of Manchukuo (signature of the Manchurian protocol) decisively worsened subsequent relations between Japan and China. China, which had been demanding withdrawal of the twenty-one demands for the railway and other rights and privileges forced on it within its sovereign territory of Manchuria, was in contrast quite unable to accept that Manchuria and Mongolia should become the de facto territory of Japan. In the period between 1931 and 1932, there were no preparations for war on the Chinese side. But the return of 'Manchukuo' to China, rather than the withdrawal of the twenty-one demands, became the uniform goal of the government and the people of China, so that the government, the armed forces and the Communist Party were preparing for a war against Japan.

In the Japanese Army, however, after the death of Yamagata Aritomo, there were no more leaders believing that 'China must not be disparaged'. At the time of the twenty-one demands to China in 1915, Akashi Motojirō, deputy-chief of the General Staff, earned the antipathy of the government and the people of China, and apparently considered only Russian and British reactions in making the policy. In the Manchurian Incident, the army leaders paid attention to the actions of Great Britain and France in the League of Nations, as well as to the reactions of the United States and the Soviet Union, both rising powers now coming to eclipse Britain and France, but they hardly bothered about the moves of the Chinese government and people to make preparations for war against Japan. In the midst of the all-out war that followed the Marco Polo Bridge Incident on 7 July 1937, the Japanese Army had to pay the cost of its underestimation of China lasting over many years.

The London Naval Disarmament Treaty

The 'Constitution' camp did not refrain from opposing the alliance between the 'Old Empire' and the 'New Empire. In the second general elections (1930) following universal male suffrage, the *Minseitō* led by Hamaguchi Osachi won a major victory promoting the need for naval disarmament and non-interference in the domestic affairs of China. It is well known that the *Minseitō* of Prime Minister Hamaguchi, who had taken seriously the 'will of the people' in the elections, overcame opposition from Katō Hiroharu, chief of the Naval General Staff, who was hiding behind the shield of 'independent access to the Throne' (*tōsuiken*), and concluded the London Naval Disarmament Treaty.

In this process, however, the *Minseitō* Cabinet acted in such a way as to end up defending the 'independent access to the Throne' on the part of the High Command.

What the Naval High Command was advocating was that the independent access to the Throne was not just confined to military strategy as designated in article 11 of the Meiji Constitution. They argued that it also included decisions on the amount of military equipment necessary for national defence, as in the 'Imperial Defence Policy' (Constitution, article 12). They insisted that the military disarmament treaty deciding the ratio of warships between the four powers of Great Britain, the United States, France and Italy fell within the ambit of the 'Independent access to the Throne', and that the Disarmament Treaty that had ignored the opinions of the Naval High Command, and had failed to protect the ratio for large cruisers of 70 per cent by comparison with Great Britain and the United States, was invalid. The Old Empire faction of the opposition, *Seiyūkai*, supported this position of the High Command, and fiercely criticized this 'infringement of the independent access to the Throne'.

The Hamaguchi Cabinet on this issue outsmarted the Naval High Command, which signed the London Naval Disarmament Treaty, and also overcame criticism from the Privy Council (*Sūmitsuin*). The 'Empire' line being taken by the navy, seeing America as the potential enemy and pursuing rearmament, was not the same as the 'New Empire' line of the army which, starting with Manchuria and Mongolia, was aiming at the Chinese mainland, but we may say that this was a victory of 'Constitution' over 'Empire'.

Nevertheless, in the process of winning, the *Minseitō* Cabinet fell into the predicament of paradoxically emphasizing the 'Independence of military operations' for the *Kantōgun* and other local units stationed abroad. A kind of defence policy based on naval disarmament, unlike the strategic command of forces on the ground, did not belong to the independent access to the Throne, and since they insisted on being under the aegis of the cabinet, surprisingly it was a liberal party cabinet that promoted the independence from the cabinet of local forces' strategic command.

Failure of the policy of not allowing the affair to spread

It was in September 1931 that the *Kantōgun* on its own dramatic initiative committed the act of blowing up the Manchurian Railway at Liutiaokou in a suburb of Hōten (Mukden), and advanced to Chichihar in the north and to Jin (Japanese = Kin) Province in the south. At this time also, Wakatsuki Reijirō, heading the *Minseitō* Cabinet that succeeded that of Hamaguchi, together with his foreign minister, Shidehara Kijūrō, put all their effort into checking the delinquent behaviour of the *Kantōgun*. Explaining the strong reaction from Western countries, including the United States, they made the chief of the General Staff, Kanaya Hanzō, issue a constraining order against further military activity by the *Kantōgun*.

When the chief of the General Staff issued a restraining order against military activity, it could be handled in the form of an 'order sanctioned by the Emperor', within the ambit of the independent access to the Throne. In fact, Foreign Minister Shidehara received the cooperation of Minami Jirō, the army minister, and up to this point they were able to restrain any further spread of the Manchurian Incident.

The 'Imperial Order', however, took some time to act as a restraint. In the meantime, the American secretary of state, Henry Stimson, began to lose patience. I will cover the details of this as one of my studies of specific events in Chapter 10, but the real problem was that Stimson, after his first explosion of anger, received a protest from the Japanese ambassador to the United States, and this was at an explanatory press conference. He explained that his expression was not an attack on the Japanese government, but that he was only emphasizing his belief in Shidehara diplomacy based on a report he had received from the American ambassador in Japan (a firm promise 'to curb further delinquent behaviour on the part of the *Kantōgun*'). On this occasion, Stimson affirmed in a public presentation that the content of the 'firm promise' was that 'the pledge by Japan constituted a clear promise from both the civilian and military authorities', and that 'the Japanese Government had issued an order to the same effect to the Japanese military commander in Manchuria'.

Unlike an American president, a Japanese prime minister lacked the power to issue a direct order to the 'military commander'. At the time of the conclusion of the London Naval Disarmament Conference a year earlier, the *Minseitō* Cabinet had reaffirmed the 'independent access to the Throne' on this point alone. Therefore, Foreign Minister Shidehara entrusted the curbing of the *Kantōgun* to Kanaya, chief of the High Command, through Minami, the minister for war. But through this statement by the American secretary of state, the chief of the High Command, Kanaya, lost his ability to curb the *Kantōgun*, and the foreign minister, Shidehara, was coming to have to carry the responsibility for interference in matters relating to the Privilege of the High Command (infringement of independent access to the Throne), as well as for leaks concerning issues about this privilege. It became impossible to maintain a policy of not allowing the Manchurian Incident to spread. 'Constitution' was defeated in favour of 'Empire.'

The 5-15 Incident and the death of party cabinets

We often hear that the Manchurian Incident occurred in the midst of an advancing trend towards economic blocs brought about by the Great Depression that originated in the United States. However, in March 1928, Lieutenant-Colonel Tōjō Hideki and Major Ishiwara Kanji from the core of the army expressed the need 'to establish complete political control over Manchuria and Mongolia', which was a year and a half before the beginning of the Great Depression. The idea that aggression committed by their own country was caused by world trends flies in the face of history. Moreover, at the time when Tōjō was calling for a takeover of Manchuria and Mongolia, he argued that 'Military preparations by the National Army are mainly premised on a war with Russia, and war with China does not require much consideration'. The idea of China as a 'potential enemy', as maintained by Yamagata at the time when the 'Imperial Defence Policy' was being drawn up after the Russo-Japanese War (discussed in Part II), was now being forgotten.

The point that it had nothing to do with the Great Depression was also true of the 5-15 Incident. The popular view that the young naval officers engaged in terrorist activities out of sympathy for farmers suffering as a result of the Great Depression, and having to sell their daughters into prostitution, is widespread even today.

However, in the diary of the principal instigator of this incident, First Lieutenant Fujii Hitoshi (a selection from a year's entries between January

1931 and January 1932), there is absolutely no reference to the travails of farmers suffering as a result of the Depression.[1] What emerges instead is the record of the idea of a 'revolution', and the means of bringing it about, through insurrection by young officers, by overthrowing the party cabinet and replacing it with a military cabinet. Fujii compares his role with that of the leaderless samurai of the Mito domain, seen as the harbingers of the Meiji Restoration having killed in 1860 the Chief Minister Ii Naosuke outside the Sakurada Gate (of the Imperial Palace), and proclaiming the opening of the country.

It is true that around 1930 the world Depression exerted a momentous influence on the Japanese society and economy, and thus on the lives of ordinary people. But it had no direct relationship with the Manchurian Incident and the 5/15 Incident, both of which occurred for their own specific reasons.

The 'Constitution' faction suffered a severe blow from a series of actions by the army and navy. The *Minseitō* Cabinet was forced to resign as a result of the Manchurian Incident, and the *Seiyūkai* Cabinet that replaced it fell following the 5/15 Incident. Between the resignation of the *Seiyūkai* Cabinet of Prime Minister Inukai in 1932 and the defeat of Japan in August 1945, not a single-party cabinet made its appearance.

In a series of previous publications this writer has argued that even following the demise of party cabinets and the establishment of Manchukuo, efforts were being made to revive 'Constitution', and that a real possibility existed that the trend towards 'Empire', from the Manchurian Incident to the outbreak of total war between Japan and China in 1937, might be blocked. Examples of this are *Shôwa shi no ketteiteki shunkan* (*Decisive Moments in Shôwa History*)[2] and *Nihon kindai shi* (*Modern Japanese History*).[3]

In this book I have followed this interpretation, but on one point I need to make a minor correction. As a result of surveying modern Japanese history placing the emphasis on the clash between 'Empire' and 'Constitution', I have been forced to focus on the extent of difference between whether the 'Constitution' side was controlling the cabinet, and whether, having lost control of the cabinet, it depended entirely on the House of Representatives.

In the 'cabinet' rested the decision-making power over defence and foreign policy, except for the right of independent access to the Emperor by the armed forces. This was why the *Minseitō* Cabinet of Hamaguchi Osachi was able to overcome opposition from the Naval High Command, signed the London Naval Disarmament Treaty, and was able to ratify it.

Under national unity cabinets, however, after the shooting of Inukai Tsuyoshi, no party president became prime minister. No party, whether it was the *Seiyūkai* or the *Minseitō*, was able to directly control defence and foreign policy. Shidehara, who was foreign minister in the second cabinet of Wakatsuki Reijirō that followed that of Hamaguchi, made a request to the defence minister, and prevailed on him to issue an Imperial Order preventing an advance into Jin (Japanese = Kin) Province (see p. 193) but that was only possible because the prime minister was also a party president. Such was the strength of prime ministerial power.

This being the case, if we look at the results, over the thirteen years from then until the 1945 defeat, 'Constitution' lost the power to defeat 'Empire', since party cabinets came to an end with the 5/15 Incident.

This, however, is history seen from the perspective of its results, and up until the 2-26 Incident of 1936, the *Seiyūkai* and the *Minseitō* had not abandoned their ambition to return to power. In the general elections of 20 February 1936, the *Minseitō* made substantial progress, and although it did not attain a majority, its dream of returning to power was beginning to be realized.

The influence of the 2-26 Incident

The 2-26 Incident, however, completely wrested from them the possibility of reviving a party cabinet. On 26 February, a mere six days after the elections, eight companies of the Palace Guard Division, the Infantry Regiment of the First Division stationed in Tokyo, and the field operations Heavy Artillery Regiment, totalling 1,485 officers and men, conducted an insurrection, attacking the offices, private residences and other locations of Prime Minister Okada Keisuke, the home minister, the former home minister, the head chamberlain, the minister of finance and the chief of army education. Among them the Lord Keeper of the Privy Seal, Saitō Makoto, the minister of finance, Takahashi Korekiyo, and the education chief, Watanabe Jōtarō, were all attacked at home in the early morning and lost their lives.

With the exception of Watanabe, they were all known as 'Senior Statesmen' (*jūshin*). They had been entrusted by the Emperor to choose successive prime ministers, together with the Senior Statesman (*Genrō*) Saionji Kinmochi. The young officers who conducted the insurrection intended to construct an army cabinet, appointing as Prime Minister Masaki Jinzaburō, a former inspector-general of education. In order to bring this about, they intended to replace the senior statesmen. Their reason for shooting the education chief was apparently because he was the successor to Masaki who had been forced to resign the post.

The Emperor, whose trusted senior statesmen had been attacked, was manifestly angered, and went so far as to say that he would lead the Palace Guard, which he headed, to suppress the insurrectionary force. The strong determination of the Emperor prompted the vacillating army leadership to pull itself together, and in the early morning of 29 February, the 24,000 men of the Palace Guard, 1st and 14th divisions, were ordered to deploy in order to suppress the insurrection. Rather, less than 1,500 of the insurrectionary force surrendered, and the soldiers went back to their own units. The Company Commander Nonaka Shirō committed suicide.

In this way the 2-26 Incident itself ended in the total defeat of the insurrectionary forces. But it represented a major blow to the forces of 'Constitution'.

As the Emperor said to his Head Chamberlain: 'The killing of my old and trusted advisers feels as though I am being strangled with a silk cloth', and from this affair onwards, the power of the Emperor and his close advisers as well as their political influence sharply declined. The Emperor, who said at the time of the 2-26 Incident: 'I am prepared myself to lead the Palace Guard Division to suppress the insurrection', kept a low profile until his surrender broadcast on 15 August 1945.[4]

Counter-attacks by the forces of 'Constitution' continued, as seen in the rise of anti-war and anti-fascist opinion even after the 2-26 Incident, from the 'Army purge' speech to the Diet by Saitō Takao of the *Minseitō* in May 1936, in which he took a frankly anti-fascist and anti-militarist position, to the twentieth general election in April 1937 (Japan's final genuine general election before the war).

If, however, we are talking, not of warding off fascism, but of protecting against 'Empire' (specifically, avoiding the Japan–China War that began in July 1937), then the forces of 'Constitution' would have to organize a 'cabinet', and take the Emperor's power of making foreign policy into its own hands. Article 13 of the Great Japan Imperial Constitution states that 'The Emperor declares war, makes peace and concludes treaties', so that even in an undeclared war, sending troops to China was included in the foreign policy powers. In the official commentaries on the Constitution by its drafters, Itō Hirobumi and Inoue Kowashi,[5] it is explained that 'What is shown in this article is essentially that foreign policy matters are conducted without involvement of the Diet, by the Emperor with the assistance of his ministers'.

The minister responsible for the foreign policy powers was naturally the foreign minister. Even after the cabinet system was introduced and the Diet inaugurated, in modern Japan not only the army and navy ministers but also the foreign minister were not chosen by members of the House of Representatives.

But the foreign minister could not declare war, make peace or conclude treaties independently and without the agreement of a cabinet conference (but consulting with the Emperor). If a member of a political party became prime minister, the possibility of wielding the foreign policy power of the Emperor was clearly shown in the conclusion of the London Naval Disarmament Treaty by the cabinet of Hamaguchi Osachi. But when there was a non-party cabinet, whether or not the *Seiyūkai* or the *Minseitō* held a majority in the House of Representatives, a war between Japan and China could not be avoided. And the 2-26 Incident made it impossible to bring about a party cabinet.

The abortive Ugaki Kazushige Cabinet

In this situation, in January 1937, an order had been received from the Emperor to form a cabinet, but because of opposition from the army the order had to be withdrawn and the Ugaki Kazushige Cabinet did not take office. This 'aborted cabinet' had been the one opportunity remaining for the forces of 'Constitution'. In my previous writings I have many times pointed out the importance of the 'aborted Ugaki Cabinet'. As we have come to see in this book, in order for the forces of 'Constitution' to overcome the forces of 'Empire', it was no good simply winning a majority in the House of Representatives, but it was also essential to capture the position of prime minister. Moreover, if because of the 2-26 Incident, the road to a revival of party cabinets was fading from view, the importance of a possible Ugaki Cabinet was coming into sharp focus.

The army veteran and governor of Korea, Ugaki Kazushige, had no direct connection with political parties, nor was he one of the Senior Statesmen, who had been targeted in the 2-26 Incident. In addition, through the difficult period for political parties that followed the 5-15 Incident, a movement of alliance between the *Seiyūkai* and the *Minseitō*, aimed at wresting back control of the cabinet, was constantly in evidence, and this movement aimed to make Ugaki prime minister. If the Ugaki Cabinet had actually materialized, it would definitely have meant the formation of a cabinet that would have been very similar to a party cabinet.

The Marco Polo Bridge Incident and despatch of three Japanese divisions

On 7 July 1937, half a year after Ugaki's failure to form a cabinet because of army opposition, the Marco Polo Bridge (Chinese Lukouchiao, Japanese *Rokōkyo*)

Incident occurred, and on the 27th the Japanese government decided to send three army divisions in the direction of Tientsin and Peking. In his diary entry the following day Ugaki wrote: 'Relations between Japan and China today are in effect on the verge of a situation of war.'[6]

As I have already noted, at the time of the Manchurian Incident six years earlier, the *Minseitō* Cabinet that held the post of prime minister acted against the *Kantōgun*, which seemed about to push beyond the Manchurian Incident on the basis of the Privilege of the High Command in article 11 of the Meiji Constitution. The cabinet placed the minister for war and the foreign minister under its control, and having obtained the cooperation of the chief of the General Staff, moved to suppress irresponsible actions under the Privilege of the High Command.

Against this the prime minister at the time of the Marco Polo Bridge Incident was Konoe Fumimaro, who had no links with political parties. The *Seiyūkai* and the *Minseitō* that controlled the House of Representatives did not have the expertise that would have enabled them to interfere in national defence and foreign policy.

We still hear the view that in pre-war Japan, it was because the 'Privilege of the High Command' (independent access to the Throne) existed independently of the cabinet that the cabinet did not prevent the further expansion of the Japan–China War, but this is wholly mistaken. The Marco Polo Bridge Incident itself was a clash between the forces of Japan and China in the suburbs of Tientsin, but what allowed it to expand into full-scale war between Japan and China was that in a decision taken on 27 July the cabinet decided to send three divisions to China.

Again, the idea remains deeply entrenched that since under the pre-war Constitution, ministers of state under the prime minister were responsible *separately* to the Emperor (article 55); the prime minister and foreign minister did not have the right to interfere in the decisions of the army and navy ministers. This also, however, is a completely mistaken interpretation. In questions concerning the nation as a whole, the minister for war, the minister for the navy, the minister of foreign affairs and the minister of finance could not make decisions alone. Ever since the Constitution came into force, the way in which cabinet decisions were arrived at was through discussion at cabinet meetings.

Thus, the decision whereby Japan sent three army divisions to China to deal with a clash between armies on the ground could not be made by the chief of the General Staff and the minister for war alone, but was taken by a cabinet meeting presided over by Prime Minister Konoe.

The content of the arguments exchanged at the cabinet meeting on the 27th is not known, but the outline of the decision taken on the 20th that were its basis are set out in a publication of the war history section of the Defence Research Institute of the (post-war) Defence Agency (later Ministry).[7] This was roughly as follows:

> Foreign Minister Hirota [Kōki]: 'Since negotiations are continuing in Nanjing between the Japanese Councillor Hidaka and the Chinese Counsellor Wang, I think we should wait for a reply. But I am not necessarily against mobilisation as such.'
>
> Navy Minister Yonai [Mitsumasa]: 'Our fundamental policy is to avoid expansion [of military activities], and also, since today it seems that an agreement to cease hostilities is being signed, what ever is the point of a further mobilisation?'
>
> Army Minister Sugiyama [Hajime]: 'You are probably right, but there is no indication that this agreement has been put into force. In addition, Chinese central forces and others are massing in the direction of Peking and Tientsin. For the protection of resident Japanese and for defence of our troops, the need is urgent to send reinforcements. . . . The present situation is becoming very tense. I would like the decision on timing of the despatch of reinforcements to be entrusted to the judgement of the High Command. If we miss the right time to do this, we risk letting the chance go.'
>
> Prime Minister Konoe Fumimaro: 'I understand the opinion of the Minister for War. Circumstances are bad, but in this instance, until we know the outcome of the meeting between Councillor Hidaka and Foreign Policy Section Chief Wang, I believe we should postpone mobilisation.'
>
> Minister for War Sugiyama: 'All right. Let us do that.'[8]

Looking at this from the perspective of what transpired, the opposition to mobilizing from the prime minister, the foreign minister and the minister for the navy only lasted to that day, and in the cabinet decision taken a week later, on 27 July, despatch of three divisions in the direction of Peking and Tientsin was ratified. The important point, however, lies elsewhere. What is crucial is that the proposal of the minister for war that 'the decision on the timing of the despatch of reinforcements [should] be entrusted to the judgement of the High Command' required, in terms of process, a ruling by the prime minister in a cabinet.

This being the case, if a politician had become prime minister and strongly was determined not to allow the Marco Polo Bridge Incident to develop into full-scale war, the situation could have been quite different. If Ugaki Kazushige, who a mere six months earlier had failed in his attempt to form a cabinet, had occupied the position of prime minister instead of Konoe, might not the decision to despatch three divisions to China on 27 July have been averted? If this had happened, might not the Marco Polo Bridge Incident have been dealt with, through some kind of agreement, as merely a local struggle, so that the all-out war between Japan and China would have been avoided? The powers of a prime minister to manage cabinet decisions under the Meiji Constitution were institutionally extremely strong. Whoever it was that was prime minister, he was able to determine the fate of the nation.

Full-scale war without a war declaration

Seen from this perspective, Ugaki's policy towards China, around the time when it was decided to despatch three divisions to China, is supremely significant. In his diary entry four days before the abovementioned cabinet decision of 20 July, he wrote as follows:

> If within the present Cabinet there were men of discernment and wisdom, perhaps we might not have acted like a parent rushing to deal with a quarrel between children. However much this parent disliked the parent of the other child, he did not have to take a tough attitude and become unpopular. In short, since it is a clash between lower class people at the starting point, first of all bringing together foreign negotiations, if the other party is perverse, then by making an open statement to the world, it is possible to make a single great decision. Arguing that using a struggle at the outset as an opportunity to wield a big stick is betraying our longstanding commitment to international morality. It is regrettable that there was no such a person within the Cabinet.

Ugaki's assertion that if 'Men of discernment' and 'men of wisdom' had been in the cabinet, it would have been possible for the Japanese government to prevent a small dispute between despatched forces from turning into a head-on confrontation between Japan and China through the sending of troops, and it was not simply an exercise in hindsight by historical researchers, but a judgement made just before the decision to send three divisions on 27 July 1937. Moreover, it was a statement by Ugaki Kazushige, who only six months before had received the support of the *Seiyūkai* and the *Minseitō*, and then had even been entrusted by the Emperor with forming a cabinet. If an Ugaki Cabinet had actually been formed, and the cabinet decision had been taken on 20 July, not under a Konoe Cabinet but under an Ugaki Cabinet, the despatch of three divisions to China could probably have been avoided.

As a result of the cabinet decision on 27 July to despatch three divisions to China, Japan and China entered into total warfare without a declaration of war, and without setting a goal for resolution of the war. About four and a half years later on 8 December 1941, Japan entered into war with the United States. Investigation of important 'epochs' in the intervening period I shall leave until the next chapter, and my overview of the complex relations between 'Constitution' and 'Empire' from after the First World War now concludes for the time being.

10

Three episodes between the two world wars

First period: 'Constitution' and 'non-Empire' under the Hara Kei Cabinet

In this chapter I shall examine in some detail the relations between 'Constitution' and 'Empire' in Japan between the two wars (of which I gave an outline in Chapter 9), looking at each period in turn, and introducing historical materials.

The first period was the three years between September 1918 and June 1922 – a period in which Hara Kei and Takahashi Korekiyo served successively as prime ministers.

This three-year period was a remarkable time in which 'Constitution' almost completely overwhelmed 'Empire'. This was not the same thing as what in postwar Japan came to be known as 'peace and democracy'. What was meant by absence of 'Empire' at this period was the return to China of the former German rights to the Shandong Peninsula that had been stolen from China during the First World War in the manner of a thief taking advantage of a house fire, as well as refraining from expanding its special rights and privileges.

The word 'Constitution' was also not the same as 'democracy'. Hara and Takahashi, during the period of the *Seiyūkai* cabinets when they were successively prime ministers, stubbornly continued to oppose the introduction of a universal suffrage. It is clear that those opposing an increase in the electorate from just three million to twelve million could not be called 'democrats'.

Therefore, if we ask whether the positions of Hara Kei and others were somewhere near to the 'constitutionalism' fashionable in recent years, it would be more accurate to say that the opposite was the case. In recent years 'constitutionalism' is put forward as a means of overcoming gerrymanders. When a cabinet formed from the majority party in the Diet is constructed, it manipulates the 'logic of numbers' and does what it wants to in defence and foreign policy, contemporary 'constitutionalism' limits the scope of traditional Constitution and Democracy.

From the perspective of this 'constitutionalism', Prime Minister Hara in February 1920 dissolved the House of Representatives without having it decide for or against the universal suffrage bill sponsored by the opposition parties. In so doing, he may be said to have consulted the electorate directly by his misuse of the 'logic of numbers', and thus contradicted 'constitutionalism'. When, at the subsequent general elections in May, Hara carried off a great victory, he made an official statement in which he declared that public opinion regarded universal suffrage as premature.

From the perspective, however, of the framework of analysis that we have been using in this book of the confrontation between 'Constitution' and 'Empire', the Hara and Takahashi cabinets were without a shadow of doubt 'constitutional' and the reverse of 'imperial'. On surveying this combination of 'Constitution' and the reverse of 'Empire', it is clear that there was diametrical opposition between that period and the *Minseitō* cabinets of Hamaguchi Osachi and Wakatsuki Reijirō between 1929 and 1931.

Hara and Takahashi, in order to suppress a trend towards 'Empire', were united not only in planning a major change in the direction of foreign policy but also in having to crack down on irresponsible actions by the army in domestic politics. In the case of Takahashi, since he committed to paper his opinions on these two points, I shall introduce here what he says principally about them. One was his proposal to abolish the Central Headquarters and the other was his proposal to bring about a radical shift in policy towards China.

A fundamental shift in China policy

In this book, which has placed modern Japanese history and Japan–China relations in relation to each other, and has been analysing developments since the Taiwan expedition of 1874, I must begin with the second of these.

Since the manuscript of May 1921, titled 'An opinion concerning the establishment of economic strength in East Asia', was the product of Takahashi, who became prime minister after the tragic death of Hara Kei, its significance was different from that suggested by idealistic commentators. Most crucially it argues that, with the understanding of China, Japanese troops stationed in China 'should be withdrawn as soon as possible, and military installations in each region should be removed as quickly as possible. In Shandong as well as in Manchuria and Mongolia the upsurge of territorial and aggressive ambitions and misunderstood policies, must be urgently halted and revised'.[1] Takahashi, who was Minister of Finance and deputy prime minister in the cabinet of Hara Kei, insisted even upon the withdrawal of the *Kantōgun*.

Takahashi was not insisting on the withdrawal of Japanese forces from their encampments in China out of idealism. He had confidence in Japanese economic strength, which had grown during the Great War. The 2,000,000,000 yen of specie saved during the Great War was the symbol of this. On this point Takahashi argued as follows:

> When in the past we used to judge the power of a country to be large or small, strong or weak, the only measure employed was that of military strength, whereas today we have to calculate national power in terms of superiority or inferiority of economic strength.[2]

If it was economic, not military, strength that showed the real power of a country, it would be necessary to repair relations with China with particular concern for economic capacity. In other words, 'If we were to bring together in a general sense Japanese finance and Chinese natural resources, Japanese manufacturing expertise and Chinese labour, then by developing the economic power of East Asia and exporting goods, we may not only ripen the fruits of Japan-China co-existence but also contribute to world progress, as well as aiding the improvement of mankind.'[3]

The argument that the General Staff Office should be abolished

In this way Takahashi, who almost totally rejected hitherto existing notions of 'Empire', promoted 'Constitution' domestically for the same purpose, and was planning to systematize control of the armed forces.

In a manuscript titled *Naigai kokusaku shiken* (*A Personal Opinion on Domestic and Foreign Policy*) Takahashi put forward the item: 'Abolition of the General Staff Office', in which he developed an argument for abolition that went far beyond those of the constitutional specialist Minobe Tatsukichi and the democratically inclined scholar Yoshino Sakuzō:

> 2. Abolition of the General Staff Office. The Institution that gives foreigners the most militaristic impression of Japan is the General Staff Office. This is modelled on the pre-war German imperial system, it is a military organisation quite

separate from the Cabinet, does not belong to the Minister for War as part of the bureaucracy, occupies a position of independence and freedom, and is in a special position, not only in relation to military matters, but also in foreign policy as well as economic policy.[4]

According to Takahashi, German defeat in the First World War was because the war plan drawn up by the General Staff Office – a similar body to that of Japan when the war became drawn out – was now familiar to its British, French and other adversaries, resulting in a total loss of German ability to resist. From his understanding of the German Staff Office, Takahashi concluded as follows:

> In that case there is no need for the General Staff Office to be an independent body making military plans, and since it invites misunderstanding externally among the major powers, and domestically leads to clashes with other leaders, it ought to be abolished, Army administration should be unified and foreign policy should be overhauled.[5]

Hara Kei as prime minister had been of the same opinion in the sense of being critical of the General Staff Office, which pressed for 'independent right of access to the Throne' (*tōsuiken*). In his diary entry for 2 September in the same year (1920) in which Takahashi had written his 'statement of opinion', Hara wrote as follows:

> To some extent the General Staff Office was promoted by Yamagata Aritomo, and so does not fit the contemporary ethos. Since the present period is entirely different from that of the Emperor Meiji, promotion of the independent right of access is dangerous for the future. The Government bears the responsibility for inflicting damage on the Imperial House, This is the principle of constitutional politics, and is also good for the sake of the Imperial House. The Imperial House is not directly involved in political matters, but I think it derives satisfaction from adopting a policy of engaging in charity and making awards. But the military personnel around the General Staff Office do not understand this point, and are liable to burden the Imperial House. This is seriously mistaken.[6]

Non-recognition of the independent access to the Emperor came close to meaning the abolition of the General Staff Office, and Hara's assertion that 'the Imperial House . . . engages in charity and making awards' went way beyond the organ theory devised by Minobe Tatsukichi, even approaching the post-war system of the Emperor as a symbol. We can say that Hara, like Takahashi, favoured 'Constitution' and rejected 'Empire'.

When, however, Takahashi wanted to distribute his printed proposal to 'abolish the General Staff Office', Hara opposed this. Even so, Hara promised to show Takahashi's statement of opinion not only to the defence minister, Tanaka Giichi, but also to Yamagata Aritomo, who as elder statesman was the 'retired Shogun' of the armed forces. This being the case, he could not have been entirely opposed to it. Hara, however, was opposed to broadcasting idealistic arguments he believed in his heart but saw as impossible to implement. In his diary on the day when Takahashi met Hara, demanding permission to distribute the statement of opinion that he had printed, Hara wrote as follows:

> 15th [October]. Cabinet meeting. . . . The Finance Minister, Takahashi, has printed a personal opinion arguing that misunderstandings held by foreign countries that Japan is a militarist country should be eliminated. He has shown it to me, asking me to distribute it more widely if I see fit. I have taken a look at it, and as a result of showing it to Tanaka Giichi who was with me, I plan to show it also to Yamagata.
>
> Takahashi's proposal is to abolish the General Staff Office as well as the Ministry of Education, and to split the Ministry of Agriculture and Commerce into an agriculture ministry and a ministry of commerce and industry. Whatever may be the case with the Ministry of Agriculture and Commerce, abolition of the General Staff Office, as well as the Ministry of Education, would really be impossible, and would needlessly create opponents. This would not profit the State. At any rate, if he were to put this into practice, it would need to be decided by a cabinet resolution that avoided a plethora of difficulties. When I told him that the circulation of his personal opinion would need to be postponed, Takahashi agreed to follow what I said.[7]

In order to emphasize 'Constitution', I have refrained from discussing his proposal to abolish the Ministry of Education. But this was not so shocking as his proposal to abolish the General Staff Office.

From Hara's diary it is evident that there was a difference of nuance between them in the criticism of the 'independent access to the Emperor'.

What is important here, however, is that both Hara and Takahashi wished to make major revisions to the current line of 'Empire' externally, and for this purpose they were seeking to weaken the focus of 'militarism' domestically. The Hara Cabinet, by strengthening 'Constitution' domestically, given that it was a cabinet that previously had promoted 'Militarism in external affairs', was now in tune with the times.

It goes without saying that this combination of 'Constitution' without 'Empire' was one link in the mainstream of world opinion at that time following the First World War. But in contrast to the period after the Second World War, Japan at that time did not just passively react to 'world trends'. The Naval Disarmament

Treaty concluded at an international conference in Washington, the nine-nation Treaty relating to China, the Four Power Treaty between Japan, the United States, the United Kingdom and France, all signed between the end of 1921 and the beginning of 1922, were aimed at preventing the outbreak of another war (restrictions on the number of warships permitted for the United Kingdom, the United States, Japan, France and Italy), as well as restrictions on moving towards 'imperialism' in East Asia (termination of the Anglo-Japanese Alliance and maintenance of Chinese territory and sovereignty). At that conference Japan attempted to play one of the leading roles.

Second period: Counterattack in favour of 'Empire' under the cabinet of Tanaka Giichi

The *Seiyūkai*, which appointed the former minister for war, Tanaka Giichi, as its president in April 1925, lost power in August. But he ended the 'non-Empire' line that had persisted since the Hara Cabinet, and developed policies based on 'Empire', of maintaining special Japanese rights in Manchuria and Mongolia. As I have already shown, however, in order really to change national defence policy it was necessary to be in power. What he had achieved for the *Seiyūkai* while it was out of power was 'to encourage the Government, to awaken favourable opinions among the people and to maintain our imperial position in Manchuria'.

It is well known, however, that when, in April 1927, the *Seiyūkai*, having changed its China policy, returned to power, maintenance of special rights in Manchuria and Mongolia became the basis of its defence policy as well as of its foreign policy.

Nevertheless, even though policy had shifted to 'Empire', this was still a period of party cabinets. When the opposition *Kenseikai* (later *Minseitō*) replaced the *Seiyūkai* in power, a further change in China policy became possible. Indeed, when, two years later in July 1929, a *Minseitō* Cabinet under Hamaguchi Osachi replaced the *Seiyūkai* Cabinet of Tanaka Giichi, the policy of non-interference in Chinese internal affairs, and in favour of Japan–China friendship, was once again emphasized. In his first official speech after taking office Hamaguchi, beginning with the policy towards China, spoke as follows:

> Concerning Empire and relations with our neighbour, China, our Government's policy is nothing other than to establish eternal friendship based on co-existence and co-prosperity between our two countries.

As is clear from these things under the system (habit) of two major parties, while the conservative party could implement 'imperialist' policies, when the progressive party came back to power it was able to return once again to 'non-imperial' policies.

The plan to take over Manchuria and Mongolia

As we have already made clear, Japanese 'Imperialism' was different from 'war', and the problem concerned the right of independent access to the Emperor, upon which the General Staff Office had been continually insisting. It would have been different if Takahashi's idea of abolishing the General Staff Office had been implemented, but in the case of policy towards Manchuria and Mongolia, the cabinet would not do anything about the behaviour on the ground of the *Kantōgun* without going through the General Staff Office. Given such a system of control, 'non-imperial' policies of progressive cabinets had their limits.

A progressive cabinet, using article 13 of the Meiji Constitution, 'The Emperor declares war, makes peace and concludes treaties',[8] could probably have prevented full-scale war with China, but so far as the behaviour of the troops deployed was concerned, because of the problem of the independent power of access to the Emperor in article 11,[9] the cabinet would not have been able to exercise direct control. Under this pre-war constitutional system, the activities of the military substantially determined whether the outcome would be 'Empire' or 'non-Empire'.

From this perspective, the 'significant period' in which the suppression of 'Empire' by 'Constitution' was brought to an end may be considered the beginning of the plan by middle-ranking army officers to take over Manchuria and Mongolia during the period of the Tanaka Cabinet. These were not young officers, but principally colonels, lieutenant-colonels and majors, in other words middle-ranking army officers, who formed a study group called the Thursday Society (*Mokuyôkai*), where they resolved to take over Manchuria and Mongolia. In the records of the Thursday Society left by Major Suzuki Teiichi, there is no record left of the group's first meeting, but there were monthly meetings from the second meeting on 1 December 1927, to the sixth meeting on 5 April 1928, and then after a hiatus of about six months the record of meetings resumed from November 1928 to February 1929.

This study group, consisting of middle-ranking officers from the Ministry for War and the High Command, included names familiar to any Japanese with an interest in the Shōwa period history: Nagata Tetsuzan (Colonel), Tōjō Hideki (Lieutenant-Colonel), and Ishiwara Kanji (Major). There were eighteen of them, with the ranks of colonel, lieutenant-colonel, major and captain. In terms of the frequency of their attendance, Tōjō seems to have been the central figure. Important also was Ishiwara Kanji, who taught at the Army University, and gave a paper at this meeting on his famous *Sekai saishû sen ron* (The World's Final War). Ishiwara absented himself from the meeting on 8 November 1928, his reason being that he had been 'posted to the *Kantōgun*'. Ishiwara, who had joined the *Kantōgun* High Command in October of the same year, at the March meeting of the Thursday Society, took very much to heart a proposal from Tōjō. And so, about three years later, in September 1931, the Manchurian Incident took place. He was reported as follows:

> For the consolidation of our Empire, we must establish total political power over Manchuria and Mongolia. For this purpose, preparation of our military forces for war should be based on the Russo-Japanese War, and it will not be necessary to concern ourselves with war with China. But if this war should take place, we must be concerned with American participation and make defensive preparations.[10]

Third period: The clash between 'Constitution' and 'Empire' over the Manchurian Incident

The decision of a middle-ranking army officer that 'we must establish total political power over Manchuria and Mongolia' was brought to fruition in the Liutiaokou (Manchurian) incident of 18 September 1931. The *Kantōgun*, starting from southern Manchuria, moved north into the Heilongjang Province and into other provinces, and finally to *Chang Cheng*, and in March 1932 appointed Pu Yi, who had been the last of the Ch'ing Emperors, to be titular ruler of Manchukuo.

This affair is probably the best-known event in Japan–China relations since the Meiji Restoration. What is important from this book's perspective is why the *Minseitō* Cabinet – with a majority in the House of Representatives, and which one year before, in 1930, had overcome opposition from the navy and put into effect the London Naval Disarmament Treaty – had not managed to suppress the *Kantōgun*.

In research into Japanese modern history hitherto, the answer to this question was clear: the independent access to the Throne by the armed forces took it out of the hands of the government.

However, as I have argued in this book so far, the power of a cabinet, and especially the power of the prime minister, even in pre-war Japan, was greater than widely imagined. Moreover, the *Minseitō* cabinets of Hamaguchi Osachi and Wakatsuki Reijirō were a match for the previously discussed *Seiyūkai* cabinets of Hara Kei and Takahashi Korekiyo, and indeed were the strongest party cabinets of pre-war Japan. Researchers have perhaps been too much constrained by the phrase 'independent access to the Emperor'. In truth, did the *Minseitō* Cabinet attempt to suppress unauthorized activity by the *Kantōgun*, but for reasons of circumstance failed in their attempt? In short, was it the case that, despite 'Constitution' trying to overcome 'Empire', the attempt resulted in failure, and the colony of Manchukuo was established?

In an article published more than thirty years ago, titled 'Diplomatic Misunderstandings and the Extension of the Manchurian Incident', I analysed the circumstances whereby Shidehara Kijūrō, foreign minister in the second *Minseitō* Wakatsuki Cabinet, obtaining the cooperation of Colonel Minami Jirō, the minister for war, and Kanaya Hanzō, chief of the General Staff, for a time succeeded in restraining the expansionist activities of the *Kantōgun*, but because of a press conference given by the US Secretary of State, Henry Stimson, this approach collapsed.

Control of the *Kantōgun* at one point succeeded

Why was it that 'Constitution' for a while succeeded in controlling the unauthorized actions of 'Empire' becomes clear from the following two sources.

The first is a document titled 'The circumstances of relations between the military and the Foreign Ministry concerning the Manchurian issue', distributed on 2 December 1931 by the second branch of the General Staff to the Association of Former Soldiers at Home. For the purposes of this book, this is an extremely important document, so I will reproduce it almost in its entirety.

> At about 19.00 in the evening of 23 November 1931, a telephone call was received by the Minister for War, Minami, from Kanaya, the Chief of the General Staff. Its gist was as follows:
>
> From various sources Foreign Minister Shidehara suspects that the *Kantōgun* is pushing forward with its incursion into Jin Province, and wishes to ascertain the situation for himself. I told him that such a situation should not develop, but if there were some special reasons to need affirmation, he had better talk to you

directly. I promised him that I would tell you about this. This being the case, I shall be happy if you would tell the Foreign Minister about the situation so far as you can.

[From the Minister for War] In respect of the above telephone call, the Chief of the General Staff telephoned about 8.00 p.m., and replied to Foreign Minister Shidehara as follows:

According to the Minister for War, the Foreign Minister has received information concerning the rapid development of the advance by the *Kantōgun* into Jin Province, and is extremely concerned, but I believe that there is no such intensification of the advance'. . . . In reply to this the Foreign Minister asked: 'Leaving aside Chinese propaganda, as far as I hear, in the name of the Deputy Chief of the General Staff, telegrams are coming from foreign embassies and military posts, telling of a rapid advance into Jin Province, so is this in fact misinformation?' To this the Chief of the General Staff replied that 'None of this is correct. However, for your information I will report later on the basis of an investigation concerning the situation in Jin Province. And he ended the call at this point'.

The Chief of the General Staff, within about an hour, having checked the information about Jin Province, once again called the Foreign Minister, and told him that: 'The activities of the *Kantōgun* in Jin Province were entirely against bandits.'[11]

The foreign minister in this party cabinet thus expressed strong concern to the minister for war concerning the further extension of the Manchurian Incident, the minister for war informed the chief of the general staff of this, recommended that he telephone the foreign minister, the chief of the general staff twice called the foreign minister and promised firmly that he would not allow the *Kantōgun* to attack Jin Province. 'Constitution' was attempting to overcome 'Empire'.

As we have already seen in the previous chapter, Ugaki Kazushige, the 'elder statesman' of the army, in July 1937 opposed the extension of a local conflict into total war. Minami Jirō, the minister for war, and Kanaya Hanzō, the chief of the general staff, had cooperated with Foreign Minister Shidehara during the Manchurian Incident six years previously, in an attempt to prevent further expansion. These were men who had risen to top positions in the army under the patronage of Ugaki. The day after Shidehara had personally phoned the chief of the general staff, the Elder Statesman Saionji despatched his close associate Harada Kumao to Ugaki with the following message: 'Saionji is extremely concerned that no project to attack Jin Province should proceed, and he requests that you exert your best endeavours to this effect.'[12]

Thus, the behaviour of the *Kantōgun* in expanding the scope of the Manchurian Incident in order to create Manchukuo was opposed by the top officials of the army at that time. They fully supported the policy of the *Minseitō* Cabinet of the time that such expansion should not take place. This was because of strong opposition from the US Secretary of State, Stimson, which lay in the background of attempts by the Japanese foreign minister, the minister for war and the chief of the general staff to prevent attacks on Jin Province. On 23 November he had sent a stern warning through the American ambassador, Forbes, to the foreign minister, Shidehara, concerning the behaviour of the *Kantōgun*. Shidehara received this warning from the US secretary of state, relayed it to the minister for war and the chief of the general staff, and gave a firm promise to the foreign minister not to invade Jin Province. The next day, the 24th, he sent this promise through Ambassador Forbes to Stimson. The circle Stimson → Forbes → Shidehara → Minami → Kanaya → Shidehara → Forbes → Stimson was now complete, and the ending of the attack on Jin Province by the *Kantōgun*, both domestically and externally, was for the time being resolved.

An unfortunate chain of small mistakes

Over more than seventy years since the end of the war, we the Japanese people, under the constant patronage of the United States, have never experienced a mistake by a foreign policy leader determining the fate of the nation. So long as the Japan–US alliance remains stable, or conversely, so long as article 9, the peace clause, of the 1947 Constitution continues to be defended, most people believe that Japanese security is protected.

In the early 1930s, however, the world including Japan faced crisis. At that point even a small case of carelessness could have fatal consequences. The reason why on 20 November 1931 attempts to stop expansion of the Manchurian Incident failed was that the defence and foreign policy ministers of Japan and the United States committed minor mistakes leading to a chain of misfortunes.

The first mistake was a rash promise made by Kanaya, the chief of the general staff. The *Kantōgun* would not so easily give up its attack on Jin Province. Between the General Staff Headquarters and the *Kantōgun* there was something analogous to the problem of 'independent access to the Throne'. If we read the following telegram sent on 28 November by the chief of the general staff himself to his deputy, who had been sent to the area, this is immediately clear. The telegram was sent five days after he had stated clearly to Foreign Minister Shidehara that he would not allow an attack on Jin Province to occur:

> Concerning the inappropriate behaviour of the *Kantōgun* in the area of Jin Province, my official opinion has been expressed in frequent telegrams, but now it is unbelievably unfortunate that the *Kantōgun* lacks the sincerity to obey central control, and also that there is disunity within the *Kantōgun* command.
>
> I ask you to convey frankly to the commanding officer and to the Chief of the General Staff the above impressions, maintain serious reflection on the matter, organise something as close as possible to an Imperial Order, so that they may receive censure for their infringements, so that they do not repeat such behaviour. This the two of them must ensure.[13]

It is difficult to evaluate this telegram from the chief of the general staff. Depending on one's point of view, the materials show that Kanaya's non-expansion policy was genuine. But on the other hand, if we look at the position of the US secretary of state, even if the firm promise on the 24th transmitted by Foreign Minister Shidehara not to attach Jin Province came to seem unreliable, that was hardly surprising. At a press conference that Stimson held on 27 November, he made the following observations:

> The Japanese promise by the civilian and military authorities that I received just three days ago was in its context an extremely clear guarantee. The American Government up to the present day has consistently believed that progress is being made towards peace.

Because of the time difference, the press conference was reported in the Japanese press in their evening editions of the 28th (the date on the newspapers was 29 November, but evening editions at that period were attached to the next day's papers). Stimson exploded with rage that the 'firm promise' made on the 24th by 'civilian and military authorities' had not been fulfilled at all.

Stimson's failure

This expression of anger that the helpful initiative by the chief of the general staff had still not been fulfilled only three days later was a mistake committed by the American Secretary of State. This was the second mistake.

The US secretary of state has the same status as a foreign minister. Just as the Stimson statement represented the American government, it was probably appropriate for the Shidehara promise to have been treated as representing the Japanese government. In spite of this, Stimson deliberately insisted that it was 'a firm promise of the civilian and military authorities'. And then, in the final part of his speech, he confirmed that 'Prime Minister Shidehara in this same reply expressed the view that the Japanese Government had already issued an ordinance targeting the Japanese military authorities in Manchuria'.

Stimson may perhaps have wished to exaggerate his degree of understanding of Japan, but it was the chief of the general staff, not the Japanese government, that could have issued orders to the military authorities in Manchuria. As I have already explained in the previous chapter, a formal declaration of war exceeded the authority of the chief of the general staff and the *Kantōgun* command, since war was decided by the cabinet. But control of the activities of troops despatched to local wars belonged to the Army Commanding Officer and the chief of the general staff, so that on this the prime minister and foreign minister had no authority. Therefore Kanaya had merely transmitted the intention of the High Command that they should not invade Jin Province, as something that Foreign Minister Shidehara had said.

The US secretary of state gave this story official status, and the Japanese evening editions reported it on their front pages under the heading 'Washington 27th, Rengō [press agency]'. For this alone Shidehara would probably have been forced into retirement.

The sole escape route for Shidehara, who in fact was left in place, was to hold a press conference and explain that this Rengō article had been wrongly reported to Stimson. In fact Foreign Minister Shidehara, through the Japanese ambassador to the United States, Debuchi Katsuji, demanded an explanation from Stimson. Debuchi failed to understand the points in the 'conversation'. Without demanding an explanation of the part of the Rengō article that dealt with the 'infringement of the independent right of access to the Throne', he directed a poorly targeted attack on Stimson. We are not fully aware of the nature of the ambassador's criticism of Stimson. However, it is clear from Stimson's press conference that its content was miscalculated. The press conference was reported in the Japanese press on the 29th:

> Concerning my statement at the press conference that you attended on the 27th, if you have a record of it, that is sufficient. As is clear from the record, things that I never said on that day, and things that I have never said at all were completely misreported to the Japanese Foreign Ministry.

It is clear that what Debuchi was attacking he did not refer to at the press conference, and what he referred to on the 27th were two points, no matter in which order:

> In reply, on the following day, the 24th, I received from Foreign Minister Shidehara through Ambassador Forbes clarification that the Foreign Minister, the Minister for War and the Chief of the General Staff were united in their opinions and that the locally deployed Command had been ordered not to engage in military movements towards Jin Province. (Since I myself believe this statement, I do not need to issue statements confirming it).

Breakdown of the non-expansion policy

As is clear on the first reading, Stimson deliberately corrected his statement, specifying the points that he wanted the Japanese government to delete. These were the independent access to the Throne embodied in article 11 of the Constitution, and that the *Kantōgun* answered to the orders only of the chief of the general staff. If this order was issued following consultation with the minister of foreign affairs, then the chief of the general staff would have infringed the 'independent access to the Throne'. The content of telephone discussions between the foreign minister and the chief of the general staff, which was undoubtedly an internal consultation, was disclosed at the press conference of the secretary of state, and when this was reported in extra editions of Japanese newspapers, it was a mortal blow to Foreign Minister Shidehara. Shidehara immediately sent a protest in the following terms to Ambassador Forbes. It was, however, not so much a protest as something close to a report that the policy of preventing an expansion of the Manchurian Incident had failed.

> The report transmitted by Associated Press (AP) as a record of the press interview that the Secretary of State gave to reporters, has had a profound effect. The fact that Your Excellency revealed the internal circumstances of the order to the High Command of the forces in Manchuria issued by this Minister that the military should refrain from advancing into Jin Province has repeatedly been the subject of attention. It was meant strictly as an internal secret for Your Excellency and for the American Government, and I never expected that the Secretary of State would inform the press of this. Because such confidential material was released, this Minister [Shidehara] is receiving fierce attacks from the military authorities and from public opinion, and his own position is in jeopardy.[14]

It was not only Shidehara who had totally lost face over this matter. The chief of the general staff, Kanaya, as well as the minister for war, Minami, were similarly affected. Both the Foreign Ministry and the Army High Command had no choice but to give the green light to an advance into Jin Province. On 7 December, a telegram was sent by the minister for war to the *Kantōgun* and to troops stationed in China; the Army Ministry and the Foreign Ministry both revealed that they had shifted to the 'overriding foreign policy power' in article 13 of the Constitution, thus accepting activities within the scope of the 'independence of access to the Throne' for the 'clearing out of bandit elements', as well as military engagement with the Regular Chinese Forces.[15]

The meaning of this telegram may be summarized in three points.

The first point is that it was sent, not in the name of the chief of the general staff, but in the name of the minister for war, to the *Kantōgun* and to the troops stationed in China. Second, in it the minister for war made clear that the content of the telegram had been completed 'in an arrangement with foreign policy officials'. Third, it not only approved 'clearing out of bandits' but also 'military engagement with Chinese forces'. This meant the total collapse of the foreign policy towards China conducted by the Shidehara foreign policy under the second Wakatsuki Cabinet, which had blocked the advance into Jin Province, with cooperation between the foreign minister, the minister for war and the chief of the general staff. Four days later, on 11 December 1931, the second Wakatsuki Cabinet resigned. 'Constitution' had been defeated by 'Empire'.

Extinction of 'epochs'

At a time when the urban populations and the parliamentary forces were active in their demands for democratization, Japanese expansion in China came to a halt. Moreover, the forces of Constitution, up to the eve of the outbreak of war, were anti-war, or war-weary. But to overcome, not war in general, but military invasion of China was not so much a public opinion or parliamentary matter, but required the cabinet to come to grips with its sovereign power over national defence and foreign policy. Even so, there are times when 'Imperialism' cannot be effectively held at bay, and there is no means of preventing in advance aggressive war without taking over a cabinet. This is a key lesson from the Manchurian Incident.

This being the case, following the resignation of the *Seiyūkai* Cabinet of Inukai Tsuyoshi after the terror episode perpetrated mainly by young naval officers, there was not a single-party cabinet in the thirteen years from then until the defeat in August 1945, so that an 'epoch' during which 'Constitution' had overcome 'Empire' could hardly exist.

This, however, is to see things starting from the result, whereas people at the time were tired of the Manchurian Incident being criticized as 'Empire', and the 5/15 [1932] Incident was not seen as meaning the end of party cabinets. And then even after the Incident on 26 February 1936, nearly four years after the 5/15 Incident (a coup d'état attempt by young army officers on a much larger scale), neither the Diet nor public opinion abandoned anti-fascist arguments.

The *Minseitō*, which defeated the *Seiyūkai* at the nineteenth general elections on 20 February 1936, became the largest party, and even after the attempted coup by young army officers six days later continued to raise the anti-war and anti-militarism flag. The anti-militarist speech by Saitō Takao in May of the same year is famous. Movements of opinion exercised an influence on the conservative *Seiyūkai*, and in the 70th Diet session Hamada Kunimatsu of the same party severely criticized Terauchi Hisaichi, the minister for war, on the grounds that behind military activity lay 'Fascism' and 'authoritarian thought'.

Pressed by anti-war and anti-Fascist voices in the *Minseitō* and *Seiyūkai*, the Ugaki Kazushige Cabinet project had supporters within both parties and in part of the army.

The circumstances whereby this cabinet proved abortive are well known. On 25 January 1937, Ugaki, who had received from the Emperor the order to form a cabinet, was forced on the 29th to surrender the powers given him by the Emperor, because three army chiefs of staff (the chief of the general staff, the governor of education and the previous minister for war) refused to sponsor the next minister for war.

The upsurge of the *Shakai Taishūtō* (Social Masses Party)

In several publications hitherto, the present writer has argued that even after the failure of the Ugaki Cabinet, the activities of various forces aiming at democratization actually expanded. The doubling of seat numbers of the Social Masses Party after the twentieth general elections on 30 April 1937, and the upsurge of that party in city assembly elections in May and June, were taken note of.

This Social Masses Party, which was a legal Socialist Party, proclaimed 'broad-based defence' in alliance with the military. The party argued that 'narrow defence', focusing only on improving military preparations, was useless, and that at the same time there was a need for 'broad-based defence' to save workers struggling under pressure from capitalists seeking private profit, and also to save poor farmers. Putting this in contemporary terms, its position was to link together reduction of inequalities and improvements in military preparedness.

Ironically, however, the lower classes and progressive intellectuals of the period wanted the party to focus on opposing fascism. Tosaka Jun, the socialist philosopher of the time, evaluated it positively: 'Given the discrepancy between the huge military budget and the budget to stabilise people's livelihoods, it was the Social Masses Party that pressed the conflict between "narrow defence" and "broad-based defence".[16] Tosaka also concluded that the SMP advance in the city elections held throughout the regions following the general elections on 30 April and up to June showed that 'liberalism and democracy represent the political common sense of the Japanese people'.

Tosaka concluded his short essay by writing that democracy was trampled underfoot by the 'physical energy' of the Japan–China War.

How can democracy stop war?

On the one hand, in Japan up to June 1937, democratic forces continued to make progress. This is a historical fact. On the other hand, after the beginning of the Japan–China War the voices of democratic forces became hidden. This is also a historical fact that is clear when we see the sudden shift in editorial approach of the general magazines of the period.

Even though this was the case, the Japan–China War broke out when democracy was at its peak, and this war stifled democracy. For nearly twenty years the present writer has found it difficult to digest this apparently comprehensible, but in fact incomprehensible, story. It was not the case that war broke out after a dictatorial military regime had stifled democracy. Even so, democracy was not able to defend against the outbreak of war. Nor was the war that broke out capable of stifling democracy. However many times I rewrote the story, I was unable to escape from this circularity.

The answer, however, was extremely simple. First of all, so long as there was no war, democracy could not be suppressed. Second, once war had broken out, it was not the turn of democracy until the war was over. With these two things as premises, the issue boils down to the following single point, namely, how can democracy bring war to an end?

In fact, at various places in this book, I have managed to answer this question. If I may summarize this in a few words, when the forces of democracy come to power, they can stop war.

Article 13 of the Great Japan Imperial Constitution is often called the 'foreign policy prerogative', but this is a term that readily invites misunderstanding. Cognate expressions are 'national defence' and 'foreign policy power'. Not only declaration of war, making peace and concluding treaties, but also despatch of forces onto the territory of other countries as well as involvement in their rights, corresponding to a declaration of war, all follow from article 13 of the Constitution. As I have frequently pointed out, decisions relating to article 13 take place as decisions of the cabinet. This being the case, activities of the *Kantōgun* and the *Tientsingun* (both Japanese forces operating in China), by contrast with local wars conducted on the excuse of 'self-defence', could not rely on the 'independent access to the Throne' stated in article 11.

Putting this another way, under universal male suffrage electors send democratic forces to the House of Representatives, and when a politician from a progressive political party, or a politician corresponding to that description, accedes to the position of prime minister, then the kind of circularity into which Tosaka Jun fell could be avoided. Democracy overcomes war, and therefore a developing virtuous circle can only emerge under a liberal party cabinet or a cabinet that corresponds to that model. The reason for attaching 'liberal' to 'party cabinet' is because, as I have already explained, the *Seiyūkai* Cabinet that followed the Hara Kei and Takahashi Korekiyo cabinets came to adopt a position of recognizing 'Empire'.

This book, which has re-examined modern Japanese history following the Taiwan expedition of 1874, using the axis of 'Empire' and 'Constitution', has had to make a break with the beginning of the Japan–China War in July 1937. Once total war began, democratic forces were suppressed, and could only fall into silence. It is well known that when total war ended in August 1945, democracy returned.

Conclusion

Irresponsible 'Empire' without 'Constitution'

Points and lines

When the Ugaki Cabinet was aborted in January 1937, control of 'Empire' by party cabinets or quasi-party cabinets became impossible. 'Public opinion' was increasingly demanding 'democracy', as shown in later general and local elections, but since public opinion did not control the cabinet, it did not possess the means to stop troops being sent to China. Thus, as soon as war really began, public opinion shifted at quite an incredible speed from 'anti-war' and 'war-weary' to 'pro-war'.

This situation definitely gave a free hand to the army and other forces, which planned to expand 'Empire' from Manchuria and Mongolia to China proper. As for the overriding defence and foreign policy power embodied in article 13 of the Constitution, at a time of party cabinets the army (minister) could be resisted with the support of the Diet and of public opinion, but at a time when the prime minister and the cabinet had no such inclination to resist, countervailing power against 'Empire' was lacking. The Japanese Army, having been given a free hand, occupied Nanjing in December 1937, in May 1938 took Xuzhou Province, and in October captured Hankow.

Some time ago, when I found Matsumoto Seichō's detective story *Ten to sen* (Points and Lines), I was reminded by the author of aspects of the Japan–China War. The history of the Japan–China War that the author's generation learned after the Pacific War would have emphasized the fragility of the victories won by Japanese forces, over the 'points' (large cities such as Peking, Nanjing and Hankow) and the 'lines' (military roads that were the only other areas the Japanese troops were able to hold). In post-war Japanese historical research, 'points and lines' was an expression designed to pour scorn on the 'military achievements' of the Japanese forces. This widespread view about modern Japanese history seems to have been forgotten by the Japanese people without noticing that they had forgotten it.*

---

* Translator's note: this is curiously reminiscent of the shape of territory held by ISIS from 2014 in Iraq and Syria at its largest extent.

A lengthy war of attrition – why did a peace settlement prove impossible?

Both the government and the armed forces realized the danger inherent in 'points and lines', and at times of general attack they aimed to bring about a 'peace settlement'. But at times the prime minister, and at other times the minister for war, insisted on fishing for peace conditions that would be concomitant with 'war achievements', and the government as a whole, was unable to maintain unity.

Behind the search for conditions for peace, inflated reports by the government of military achievements were issued, typically represented by the term 'announcement from military headquarters'. The people were excited by exaggerated reports of military victories, so that torchlight processions, large-scale gatherings and demonstrations were frequently held. According to popular sentiment, the only peace worthy of consideration would be the total surrender of the Chinese government.

Chinese popular sentiment, however, was even harsher, and unflinching resistance to Japan was supported by the military, the government and the people. The former Kyoto University professor Nagai Kazu, in his book *Nitchû sensô kara sekai sensô e* (*From The Japan–China War to World War*), argued that for the Chinese side the Japan–China War was not simply a war, but was a 'national liberation war'. He expressed this in the following words:

> The war aims of the Chinese side were to expel Japanese forces from Chinese territory, and from that perspective any peace settlement not premised on total withdrawal of Japanese troops was nothing but a deception, so that to yield to this meant surrender and defeat. . . . For the Chinese side defeat in a particular battle was not a substantive issue. Endurance of all possible sufferings from enemy attacks, and persistence in the will to resist, was everything, and so long as they could maintain this attitude, final victory should be in the hands of China.[1]

In so far as this was the fundamental attitude of the Chinese side, the choice for the Japanese side was either to annihilate the Chinese forces or to withdraw entirely from China. According to Nagai, the early stage choice of Japan was the first, because of which 20,000,000 Chinese soldiers were sacrificed. But about two years after the beginning of the war, they chose, not the second path, but a third path that was the worst of all. The Japanese military, government and people, who gave up the idea of annihilating China, now opted instead for a lengthy war of attrition, and between July and August 1939, in Kōbe, Ōsaka, Yokohama,

Tokyo and elsewhere, gatherings and demonstrations of around 100,000 were held repeatedly in an attempt to destroy the British, who were backing China.[2]

However pitiless and unforgiving the invasion might have been, a mass movement calling for violence against the Chinese military and people, in circumstances of wartime nationalism, can to some extent be understood. But a mass movement that, rather than focusing on the China of that time, acted with the goal of attacking Britain that was backing China, and was able to assemble around 100,000 people, was something that surpasses my ability to understand. According to Nagai, the numbers participating in the movement exceeded 1,500,000, while those who took part in demonstrations were more than 600,000.

When we consider the desire among the military and civilians in both countries to continue the war, the scope for establishing a peace settlement seems to have been absent from the very beginning. But since the Chinese side would neither accede to a peace settlement, nor surrender, then if the Japanese side, which continued to wage war and score victories, had sued for peace or withdrawn its troops, it would inevitably have suffered follow-up attacks. If we consider these matters, at the point where Japan occupied Hankow at the end of 1938, the fact that the Japanese Army suspended its attack strategy and switched to a lengthy war of attrition at first sight appears to have been inevitable.

The leaders of each country, however, following the attitudes of their domestic armed forces and civilians, and given that both were concerned with territorial issues, could only continue the war. Both sets of leaders were obliged to incite heroic deeds, and also to grapple genuinely with the question of a peace settlement. It may be precisely this that is the duty of a statesman. As for the Japan–China War that raises these questions, Japan had started to tackle them, and those most responsible for their resolution were the Japanese prime minister, the foreign minister and the minister for war.

The Japanese people became a different people

The last chance for a peace settlement came before the attack on Hankow. After the occupation of Hankow, even though the Japanese forces held back from further attacks, the only course open to the Chinese forces was to stake everything on a scorched earth policy and fight with all their strength. Following the outbreak of the Japan–China War, an old Asianist, Ogawa Heikichi, who since the Meiji period had continued to create definitions of a peace settlement for the prime minister, the foreign minister and the minister for war, on a visit to Hong Kong in March 1939, obtained the impression that 'a desire to wage war amidst great rejoicing flourishes exceptionally, and just as in our country, they demand that those advocating peace should be killed'.[3]

Ogawa became known as an Asianist when under Konoe Atsumaro, father of Konoe Fumimaro, he worked hard to found the *Tōa Dōbunkai* (East Asia Same Script Society). Of course the country using the same script in East Asia as Japan (using the same characters) was China. Konoe Atsumaro and Ogawa insisted that Japan was protecting China from the Western Great Powers. As for Japan, which had been victorious in the Sino-Japanese War of 1895, and consistently took a victor's standpoint, it was Konoe Atsumaro and Ogawa who argued that it was defending China from the Western Great Powers. Even though they spoke of the 'Western Great Powers', yet in concrete terms, as I have pointed out repeatedly in this book, this meant Russia, with which Japan was contesting rights of control over Manchuria and Mongolia.

For Ogawa, the Manchurian Incident of 1931, rather than being a matter of relations between Japan and China, was a question of Japan–Soviet relations, and in order to prepare against Soviet Russia, he thought that Japan ought to control the whole of Manchuria, also believing that this was compatible with friendship between Japan and China.

The all-out war, however, that began in July 1937 between Japan and China, was from Ogawa's position impossible to understand or to tolerate. Fortunately or unfortunately, after Konoe Fumimaro, the elder son of Konoe Atsumaro, whom Ogawa had known since the younger Konoe's youth, was sworn in as prime minister, a full-scale war between Japan and China erupted. For Ogawa, the fact that Konoe Fumimaro, who had become Japan's highest representative and was Ogawa's old acquaintance, had authorized the despatch of divisions to China, and had directed troops to occupy Nanjing, was beyond comprehension.

Tōyama Mitsuru, the Asianist and mentor of Ogawa, a boss-like figure known as the 'continental *rōnin*' (the official specialists concerning Asian countries), felt very much the same way. Just before the full-scale attack on Nanjing, on 21 November 1937, in a printed paper by Ogawa titled 'My humble opinion on starting peace talks', when Ogawa presented it to some meeting or other, it was reported that Tōyama 'gave it his full support'. And then when it was converted into an informal talk, Ogawa wrote on the cover the following:

> I think that the people are agitated. Without Kido, Ōkubo and others, this will be difficult to implement. Tōyama is upset that Yamagata is no longer here. This reminds me of an ancient poem: 'I would welcome the return of the old days even though I used to hate them so much then.'[4]

Ogawa and Tōyama, the most expansive advocates throughout the Meiji and Taishō periods, were nostalgic for Ōkubo Toshimichi, who settled the Taiwan expedition affair as this book has analysed, and for Yamagata Aritomo, who consistently proclaimed that China was a threat. For Japanese foreign expansionist advocates between the Taiwan expedition of 1874 and the Manchurian Incident of 1931, the circumstances following the outbreak of the Japan–China War in 1937 were beyond their comprehension. Even so, the fact that the official specialist on Asian countries and boss-like figure Tōyama Mitsuru should have felt nostalgic for Ōkubo Toshimichi and Yamagata Aritomo, and could talk about his 'nostalgia for the old days that he used to hate then' astonishes this writer. The Japan–China War was a war that ought not to have been started, and the Japanese people that sang its praises during the eight years from 1937 to 1945 were, I think, a completely different Japanese people from the Japanese people both before and after that war.

Peace settlement opinion

Ogawa, who rolled back this kind of despairing opinion, supported by his old comrades such as Tōyama, and dependent on the warm friendship of Prime Minister Konoe Fumimaro from the time of his father Atsumaro, had continued to advocate peace between Japan and China. Ever since the Chinese Revolution of 1911, there were assets in the form of friendly relations with the senior officials of the Kuomintang Party of China. If the Japanese government accepted their proposals, Ogawa was prepared to be a bridge with his old friends in China who formed the core of the Chiang Kai-Shek regime.

This peace settlement opinion, attached to the Ogawa discourse (21 November 1937), began with the phrase: 'War is easy, peace is difficult. But the most difficult thing is to grasp the opportunity for a peace settlement.' The most important points in the opinion were as follows.

First, if the Chinese capital, Nanjing, should fall, this would be a most difficult circumstance for a peace settlement, and therefore obviously if there was a proposal for a peace settlement from the Chinese government, or if there were any offer of mediation from a third country, this should be followed up 'without hesitation'. The reason he gave for this could have been immediately understood by anyone, *except* for those Japanese who were in Japan over the eight years from the beginning of total war with China in July 1937 to the Japanese defeat in the Pacific War in August 1945.

He wrote as follows:

> I must say that in the fighting up to the present our rights of self-defence have been maintained. Moreover, the fall of the capital (Nanjing) and the continuous attacks on all the Chinese forces, both spiritually and physically, may be said to have sown the seeds of chastisement. Also, I should say that the advances of our forces are for me encouraging, although I fear they may fall into an enemy trap.[5]

For Ogawa, the aim of military advances was nothing other than 'to maintain our rights of self-defence'.

Second, if circumstances made it difficult for the Chinese side to propose a peace settlement, then he thought it would be fine for them to receive such a proposal from the victorious Japanese side. In his words:

> For the weaker side that is losing, it may feel shameful to open negotiations, and if Japan as leader of the east is victorious, . . . then in such circumstances a proposal, much like an announcement of surrender, would not of course mean receiving humiliation from others.[6]

Third, in January 1938, Prime Minister Konoe, apparently anticipating the statement that 'Hereafter we do not treat the Kuomintang Government as a negotiating counterpart', announced that 'If our counterpart in peace negotiations is a plenipotentiary of the Chinese Government, it does not matter who that is'. The Konoe statement was made on 16 January 1938, and Ogawa's statement of opinion was made on 21 November 1937. Ogawa reasoned as follows:

> It is normal practice from the past that he who is responsible for the [conduct of] the war should be the peace negotiator. He (Chiang Kai Shek), as the present Chinese plenipotentiary, has prestige and power. If he positively accepts what we say, it should be possible to get him to implement the conditions of a peace settlement.[7]

It was the consistent position of Ogawa that if Chiang Kai-Shek was not the Chinese negotiator, then a Japan–China peace settlement would not be possible.

As Ogawa said, so long as the People's Government of Chiang Kai-Shek did not conclude a peace treaty, even if a 'Provisional Government' were set up in Peking (December 1937), and a 'Restoration Government' were established in Nanjing (March 1938), the war between Japan and China would not end. The (Japanese) government statement that 'we do not treat the People's Government as a negotiating partner' was no different from saying that the war would be continued until (the Chinese side) surrendered.

Anti-Japanese sentiment

The plan, however, for a peace settlement with Chiang as the negotiator would not stand up if Chiang would not accept to do this. After the occupation of Hankow at the end of October 1938, even Ogawa began to have doubts about its feasibility.

A short piece written by Ogawa titled 'The Conditions in Occupied Territory', in his conclusion held that, as before, if negotiations were not concluded with the People's Government, there would be no means of combating the Chinese people, who were supporting the Communist Party and strengthening their absolute determination to wage war against Japan. On reading this article, however, it seems that before arguing about the absolute determination of the Chinese people to wage war against Japan, Ogawa was acutely aware that the choice of a peace settlement between the People's Government of Chiang Kai-Shek and Japan no longer existed.

It is difficult for me to explain the details of Chinese geographical names, but you can readily feel from Ogawa's article the strength of anti-Japanese sentiment and the rapid increase in the strength of the Communist Party. This is part of what he wrote:

> As for contemporary China, for many years in the propaganda of the Kuomintang Government, in school education, in the spread of newspapers and journals, throughout the Chinese provinces anti-Japanese sentiment has been flourishing, and since the war began last year, propaganda that Japan has become the enemy, that Japan is invading China, that this war is a life or death struggle for our people, is broadcast to local mountains, villages, and remote places, throughout the land. Moreover, the animosity of the intellectual classes is most acute. The difference between the general indifference of the people as a whole to the Sino-Japanese War in 1894-5, and the current war is like the difference between clouds and mud. And in Manchuria, when Emperor Pu Yi begin his reign (in 1932 with the establishment of the State of Manchukuo) popular opinion was just the same.[8]

The important thing here is the first phrase. In research into modern Japanese history up to now, the Manchurian Incident of 1931, the Lytton Commission report in 1932 and the Japanese departure from the League of Nations in 1933 have been highlighted above all else. But the anti-Japanese sentiment and determination to resist Japan on the part of the Chinese people was powerful beyond comparison with feelings at the time of the Manchurian Incident. Despite this, the general assumption of the Japanese people about modern history has been to neglect the Japan–China War that took place over the full four years from 1937 to 1941, and make a direct connection between the Manchurian Incident of 1931 and the attack on Pearl Harbour in 1941.

The growing strength of the Chinese Communist Party

What Ogawa emphasized in his memo *Senryôchi jijô* (the situation in the Occupied Areas) was not simply the determination of the people in China to combat Japan. His interest was in the relationship between this and the Chinese Communist Party. He argued as follows:

> Recently, in all the occupied areas, bands of hungry people are wandering everywhere demanding food, those who may be called displaced persons continue to arrive, and such displaced persons are bearing weapons and plundering every district, they are blindly following such people, and with evil intent they cause disturbances everywhere. Not only that, but defeated military stragglers engage in plunder, and follow the movement to combat Japan.[9]

In contemporary parlance this means an increase in guerrilla activity. Displaced persons who were similar to mediaeval Japanese pirates (*wakō*) were supported by wanderers, and when they were 'defeated military stragglers', these 'stragglers' were thought to be Japanese soldiers.

According to Ogawa, such guerrilla activity in the occupied territories was rapidly augmenting the strength of the Chinese Communist Party. He wrote as follows:

> The situation that I have described should be seen as offering excellent quality rice paddy for the expansion of the Communist Party. They were thriving on disorder, they rode on confusion, and at an extraordinary speed they expanded their power. Even more, in Jiangxi, Fujian, Hunan, Hubei, Anhui and Zhejiang provinces, the Communist Party is already creating its Fourth Army, so these are provinces containing the still burning embers of the red bandits. Also, apart from the red bandit areas of Sichuan, Shaanxi, Gansu and Xinjiang, the province of Shanxi is an area of strong Communist influence, and determination to fight Japan has been growing more and more intense.[10]

This passage gives the impression that, apart from the areas controlled by the Chiang Kai-Shek camp, everything was under the control of the communists. The plan of Ogawa, who had written in detail about the expansion of the Chinese

Communist Party and of communist guerrillas, was that the only force capable of combating the communists was Chiang Kai-Shek's People's Government, and he kept repeating his earlier insistence that therefore a peace treaty should be signed with Chiang Kai-Shek as the negotiating counterpart. But when we read Ogawa's version of the state of affairs in China, it seems that even utilizing the power of Chiang's Chongqing government, it would be impossible to lead the Chinese people towards a peace settlement with Japan.

I am now nostalgic about the old days I used to hate so much

Though very slender, the possibility of a peace settlement existed in December 1937, before the attack on Nanjing, and in August 1938, before the attack on Hankow. At the time of the former, Ogawa and Tōyama regarded nostalgically the leadership of the elder statesmen from the Meiji and Taishō periods Ōkubo Toshimichi, Kido Kōin and Yamagata Aritomo. At the time of the latter, Ogawa published an opinion piece in which he argued: 'The fall of Hankow was the final opportunity to open peace talks.' The final short section of his opinion piece, titled *Waga kanmi* (Personal opinion), is extremely important for this book:

> We have had a series of battles and victories, and morale is now at its peak. In this situation, to discuss a peace settlement is honestly not at all easy. I think that we need even greater farsightedness and courage from our leaders, than the negotiating skills of Ōkubo Toshimichi at Peking (1874), and the Tientsin Treaty negotiated by Itô Hirobumi (1885).[11]

Whether farsightedness and courage exceeding that of Ōkubo Toshimichi and Itō Hirobumi were now available is clear without question. During the Meiji period there were also Kido Kōin and Yamagata Aritomo, making four leaders that ruled Japan, and as Tōyama Mitsuru pointed out, it was hardly a pleasant time. But when the Japan–China War became a quagmire, that Meiji era became 'lovable'.

The fact that in the midst of the Japan–China War in 1937–8, Ogawa Heikichi and Tōyama Mitsuru looked back at the China policy of the four leaders Ōkubo, Kido, Itō and Yamagata, is this book's guiding star. Starting with the Taiwan expedition of 1894, which Kido opposed and over which Ōkubo made peace with the Chinese government, this continued with the Japan–China confrontation over control of Korea between 1882 and 1885, when Itō went to Tientsin and restored relations. And this book has also developed an analysis of the reappraisal by Yamagata Aritomo of his designation of China as a potential enemy, in the background of the 'imperial Defence Policy' of 1907, following the Russo-Japanese War.

The term 'Empire' used in this book simply means expansion into China by modern Japan. And thus it was the forces of 'Constitution' that failed to prevent Japanese expansion into China, but as this book attempts to make clear, having failed, it constructed a further check on such expansion.

After the forces of 'Constitution' finally failed in July 1937, 'Empire', attempting to stop which had failed, embarked on the quagmire of the Japan–China War, and at a time when there was still no conclusion of this war in sight, in December 1941, it went ahead with the attack on Pearl Harbour. What happened afterwards is well known.

There should be no war between Japan and China

This book will conclude without touching on 'the road to the Pacific War'. The circumstances of the outbreak of war between Japan and the United States, and the processes of defeat, are of interest to many people, but most (Japanese) have a good knowledge of the history between December 1941 and August 1945, and have their own family stories to tell.

Moreover, nearly all Japanese have learned a good deal about the 'lessons of history'. As a demonstration of this, we do not hear from the lips of Japanese people, whether they are on the conservative side or on the progressive side, any talk of a war with the United States. Even the argument that the peace clause (article 9) of the Constitution should be revised, and the Self-Defence Forces ought to be upgraded to a 'Defence Army', does not develop into an assertion that Japan should enter into a war with America. Quite the contrary, it comes linked with the view that the Japan–US alliance ought to be strengthened and preparations be made against common enemies.

Since this is an important issue in foreign policy, the conservatives, being the ruling force that they are, do not clarify who the common enemy of the Japan–US Alliance is. But among private conservative groups, calls are beginning to be heard for preparations to be made against China which is threatening the Senkaku islands. The history of the Japan–China conflict over more than sixty years from the Taiwan expedition of 1874, as this book has described, is by no means just a piece of ancient history.

I think that 'Constitutionalists' and 'Constitutional Democrats', opposed to the approval of collective defence, should consider the history of conflict between Japan and China that this book has analysed. The peace movement that has been active over the seventy-two years since the end of the war has consistently opposed the idea of becoming embroiled in an American war. This tendency was seen in the movement in 2015 and 2016 opposed to collective defence legislation. The valuable proposal put forward by the student movement SEALDs, that every citizen is sovereign, was unwittingly absorbed by the old-fashioned movement against constitutional revision. In the background of this, the assertion that Japan ought not to become involved in wars of American making was clearly visible.

The security policy put forward by the Abe government, however, is designed to involve the United States in territorial questions between Japan and China. Logically speaking, it is not necessary to revise the Constitution in order to deploy the right of individual defence for the protection of Japanese territory. Collective defence is unnecessary. Just with the present Constitution and the Japan–US Mutual Security Treaty, the Senkaku islands can be defended through the right of individual defence as well as American participation in their defence.

I think, however, that in the case of a crisis between Japan and China, if the Self-Defence Forces were deployed just relying on whether the United States will defend Japan, or whether the present Constitution acknowledges the right of self-defence, this is quite unreliable as a practical question. Therefore the Abe Cabinet advocates the strengthening of the Self-Defence Forces and revision of the Constitution.

Thus, in actual practice, if a local war breaks out between Japan and China over the Senkakus, will 'Constitutionalists' and advocates of 'Constitutional Democracy' take an anti-war position in favour of peace?

As I have explained in this book, the Constitutional forces in pre-war Japan from 1874 quite stubbornly opposed any exacerbation of the Japan–China conflict. But when war broke out between Japan and China in 1937, they were not only unable to oppose it, but they became sympathetic to the war. They found it hard to maintain total opposition to a war with China that, deep down, they had failed to take seriously.

Is not the same sort of thing happening with contemporary peace activists? It is precisely this concern that directed me towards the analysis of the history of pre-war Japan–China relations. I lack this kind of concern in reflecting on relations with the United States.

If I may repeat myself, enough is already known about 'the road to the Pacific War'. But the knowledge of the Japanese people about 'the road to the Japan–China War' is extremely limited. If the Japanese people today were to become embroiled in such a war, without doubt it would not be an American war, but a war between their own country and China.

There must not be another war between Japan and China. Therefore, it is essential to be informed about 'the road to the Japan–China War', beginning with the Taiwan expedition in 1874. This has been my motivation to write this book.

In this book the parts concerning 'Empire', in other words the parts that cover the history of China policy since Meiji, owe much to information supplied by my respected friend Professor Sorai Mamoru of Hokkaidō University. Professor Sorai looked over all my personal research in this area, and encouraged me to make revisions.

Also, my structure of dividing 'Empire' into several stages, and counterposing 'Constitutional' movements to 'Empire' at each stage, was achieved through a series of discussions with Masuda Kenji, principal editor of Chikuma Shobō publishers. I want to thank both these gentlemen for their assistance.

The hero of this concluding chapter is Ogawa Heikichi, and the principal material about him is contained in *Ogawa Heikichi kankei bunsho*. Concerning this material, I am grateful for the guidance of my respected senior colleague, Professor Itō Takashi (Emeritus Professor of Tokyo University). More than fifty years ago, in 1965, he accompanied me on a visit to Ogawa's country residence, and helped me sort out Ogawa's materials. At that time I was a graduate student, my knowledge was confined to political history of the middle years of the Meiji era, and I hardly realized the significance of the Ogawa materials of the period 1935–45. I want to once more thank him for his kindness in treating me as a researcher of equal standing to himself.

Notes

The translator was unable to check details of a few footnotes before Professor Banno's untimely death

Introduction

1 Japanese, Chinese and Korean names in this book are given with surname first.
2 Yoshino Sakuzō, 'Iaku jōsō ron' (Direct Appeal to the Throne by the Military), in *Nihon seiji no minshuteki kaikaku*, Shinshigensha, 1947, p. 14 (originally in Tokyo Asahi Shinbun, 1922).
3 The Constitution of the Great Empire of Japan only states in article 55: 'The respective Ministers of State shall give their advice to the Emperor and be responsible for it', and does not make any determination in respect of 'cabinet' and 'prime minister of the cabinet'. The Diet did not, as at present, have the power to appoint the prime minister, and a cabinet system based on Diet members did not exist. As for executive power, the Emperor had supreme power, and each minister of state gave 'advice' to the Emperor, so that constitutionally the cabinet was no more than a consultative body for discussion between the individual ministers. In the cabinet system, however, whose inauguration preceded (December 1885) the Constitution, and in the semi-official interpretation of article 55 of the Constitution (Itō Hirobumi, *Commentaries on the Constitution of the Empire of Japan*, Westport, CT, Greenwood Press, 1978, reprint of 1906 edn.) important matters of state are defined as the joint responsibility of the cabinet. The Constitution needs to be understood not only in terms of the text, but also including how it worked in practice.

In legal terms, the prime minister and ministers of state did not bear direct responsibility to the Imperial Diet (House of Representatives and House of Peers), but the Prime Minister – not the Diet – was appointed by the Emperor and bore responsibility to the Emperor there were many instances where actual personnel selection was carried out by consultation with the Genrō (Elder Statesmen) and the Jūshin kaigi (Association of Senior Statesmen) as well as other extra-constitutional bodies and individuals.

As for cabinet construction, the prime minister selected candidates for each cabinet post, and the Emperor appointed them, but so far as military ministers were concerned, serving generals or lieutenant-generals were selected, so even under party cabinets the army minister and navy minister were not chosen from Diet members (under the Meiji Constitution the foreign minister was also not selected from Diet members).

Chapter 1

1. *Ogawa Heihachirō bunsho* (Documents concerning Ogawa Heihachirō), *Sanjō ke bunshō*, 50–11, vol. 2, p. 345.
2. *Ōkuma bunshō*, Waseda University, Yūshōdō film shuppan, vol. 1, p. 76.

Chapter 2

1. *Segai Inoue kō den* (Biography of Duke Inoue), vol. 2, p. 619.
2. *Kido Kōin nikki* (Kido Kōin Diary), vol. 3, p. 144.
3. *Rikken seitai juritsu no mikotonori* (Imperial Edict to Establish a Constitutional Regime); details not given in Japanese text.
4. *Rikken no jidai no owari* (The End of the Period of Establishing the New Constitution); details not given in the Japanese text.
5. *Segai Inoue kō den* (Biography of Duke Inoue), vol. 2, p. 733.
6. *Inoue Kowashi den* (Biography of Inoue Kowashi), 4th materials section, p. 47.
7. No citation given in Japanese text (probably from Fukuzawa's Collected Writings.
8. No citation given in Japanese text (probably from Fukuzawa's Collected Writings.
9. *Itō Hirobumi kankei bunsho* (Materials concerning Itō Hirobumi), vol. 1, p. 165.

Chapter 3

1. *Yamagata Aritomo ikensho* (Opinions of Yamagata Aritomo), Hara Shobō, 1966, p. 93.
2. *Fukuzawa Yukichi zenshū* (Collected Works of Fukuzawa Yukichi), Iwanami Shoten, vol. 5, p. 186.
3. Ibid., vol. 17, p. 454.
4. Ibid., vol. 5, p. 187.
5. *Kabayama Sukenori kankei bunsho* (Materials relating to Kabayama Sukenori).
6. *Fukuzawa Yukichi zenshū*, Ibid., vol. 5, p. 307.
7. Ibid., pp. 308–12.
8. Ibid., vol. 17, p. 523.
9. Ibid., vol. 10, pp. 160–1.
10. Ibid., pp. 161–2.
11. *Nihon gaikō shi jiten* (Dictionary of Japanese Foreign Policy), Ōkurashō insatsukyoku (Finance Ministry Printing Department), p. 621.

Chapter 4

1. Translated into English as Junji Banno, *Japan's Modern History, 1857-1937* (Abingdon and New York: Routledge, 2014).
2. *Meiji tennō ki* (*Life of the Meiji Emperor*), vol. 8, pp. 205–6.
3. *Teikoku gikai shūgiin gijiroku sokki* (Stenographic Record of the Proceedings of the Imperial Diet), Teikoku gikai shūgiin shiryō ka (Imperial Diet, House of Representatives, Materials Section), vol. 7, p. 253.
4. Kaneko Kentarō (ed.), *Itō Hirobumi den* (Biography of Itō Hirobumi), Tōseisha, 3 vols, 1940–3, pp. 63–4.
5. Ibid., vol. 8, pp. 481–2.
6. Ibid., pp. 59–60.
7. *Meiji Tennō Ki* (Records of the Meiji Emperor), Yoshikawa Kōbunkan, 1968–1977.

Introduction to Part 2

1. Matsuo Takayoshi, *Waga kindai Nihon jinbutsu shi* (A History of Personalities in our Modern Japan), Iwanami Shoten, 2010, p. 108.
2. *Minponshugi to teikokushugi* (People-based Politics and Imperialism), Misuzu Shobō, 1998.

Chapter 5

1. Hara Keiichirō hen, *Hara Kei nikki* (Hara Kei Diary), Vol. 2, 1965, Fukumura Shuppan. (no page number given)..
2. Banno Junji, *Meiji Kenpō taisei no kakuritsu* (The Establishment of the Meiji Constitutional System), Tokyo Daigaku Shuppankai, 1971.
3. Nakazato Hiroshi, *Keien jidai no keisei – 1900 nen taisei no jitsuzō* (The Structure of the Katsura-Saionji Period: The Essence of the 1900 System), Yamakawa Shuppansha, 2015.
4. Ibid., vol. 2, p. 91.
5. Nakazato Hiroshi, *Keien jidai no keisei: 1900 nen taisei no jitsuzō* (The Era of Katsura and Saionji: The Reality of the 1900 System).
6. Ibid., pp. 145–6.
7. Ibid., pp. 151–4.

Chapter 6

1. *Nihon gaikō shi jiten* (Historical Dictionary of Japanese Foreign Policy), p. 61.
2. Kadota Jun, *Manshū mondai to kokubō hōshin* (The Manchurian Question and Defence Policy), p. 707.
3. *Yamagata Aritomo ikensho* (Opinions of Yamagata Aritomo), p. 294.
4. Ibid.
5. Ibid., pp. 294–5.
6. Nakao Yūji, (*Shiryō shōkai*), teikoku kokubō hōshin - kokubō ni yōsuru heiryoku oyobi teikoku gun yō heikōryō Sakutei komatsu ([Source introduction]: Imperial Defence Policy – Policy Facts concerning Requirements for both Manpower and for General Principles for the Imperial Forces) *Senshi kenkyū nenpo* (Historical War Research Annual), Bōeisho kenkyū Nenpō (Ministry of Defence Research Annual), 2000, no. 3, pp. 99–100.
7. Nakazato Hiroshi, *Keien jidai no keisei: 1900 nen taisei no jitsuzō* (The Era of Katsura and Saionji, The Reality of the 1900 System), pp. 160–3.
8. Kadota, ibid., p. 705.
9. Tokutomi Sohō, *Taishō seikyoku shi ron* (A History of the Taishō Period Political Situation), p. 6.
10. *Rinji shōgyō kaigisho rengōkai giji sokkiroku* (Records of the Provisional Assembly of the Association of Chambers of Commerce), p. 17.
11. *Dai Nihon Teikoku gikai shi* (History of the Great Japan Imperial Diet), vol. 4, p. 1045.
12. *Nihon oyobi Nihonjin*, November 1912.
13. Ibid., p. 7.
14. Yoshino Sakuzō, *Gendai no seiji* (Contemporary Politics), pp. 3–4.

Chapter 7

1. *Terauchi Masatake kankei bunsho* (Materials Relating to Terauchi Masatake), 330/3, 8 December 1912, in part amended.
2. *Tokyo shōgyō kaigisho geppō* (Tokyo Chamber of Commerce Monthly), vol. 5, no. 12, vol. 6 no. 8.
3. *Terauchi Masatake kankei bunsho* (Writings relating to Terauchi Masaki), 315/9, February 1912, day uncertain.
4. *Hara Kei nikki* (Hara Kei Diary), vol. 3, p. 275.
5. Ibid., vol. 3, p. 281.
6. *Nihon oyobi Nihonjin*, 15 March 1913. It was actually published well before that date.

7 *Tokyo Shōgyō Kaigisho geppō* (Monthly Journal of the Tokyo Chambers of Commerce), vol. 6, no. 8.
8 *Takarabe Takeshi nikki: kaigun jikan jidai* (Diary of Takarabe Takeshi: Navy Vice-Minister period, vol. 2),
9 Ibid.
10 A *koku* is approximately equivalent to 150 kilograms (of rice), or enough rice to feed one person for one year.
11 *Denken Jirō nikki* (Diary of Denken Jirō), photocopy.
12 Ibid.

Chapter 8

1 Yoshino Sakuzō, *Gendai no seiji* (Contemporary Politics), pp. 78–9.
2 *Terauchi Masatake kankei bunsho* (Materials Relating to Terauchi Masatake), 315/16, 15 July 1913.
3 *Gendai no seiji* (Politics Today), p. 236.
4 Yoshino Sakuzō, *Gendai no seiji* (Contemporary Politics).
5 *Terauchi Masatake kankei bunsho* (Materials Relating to Terauchi Masatake), 315/16, entry for 15 July.

Chapter 9

1 Hara Hideo et al., *Kensatsu mitsuroku: 5-15 jiken* (Prosecutor's Secret Report: 15 May Incident), vol. 1, Kadokawa Shoten, 1990.
2 Banno Junji, *Shōwa shi no ketteiteki shunkan* (Key Moments in The History of the Shōwa Era [1926–89]), Chikuma Shinsho, Chikuma Shinsho, 2004.
3 Banno Junji, *Nihon kindai shi* (The Modern History of Japan), Chikuma Shinsho, 2012. Published in English translation as *Japan's Modern History, 1837-1937: A New Political Narrative* (Routledge, 2014).
4 Honjō Shigeru, *Honjō nikki* (Honjō Diary), Hara Shobō, pp. 275–6.
5 Itō Hirobumi, Inoue Kowashi, *Kōshitsu tenpan gikai* (Explanation of the Imperial Constitution and the Imperial House Model), Kokka Gakkai (State Academy, 1901).
6 *Ugaki Kazushige nikki* (Ugaki Kazushige Diary), Asahi Shinbunsha, 1954.
7 *Bōeichō* (*Bōeishō*) (Agency, now Ministry, of Defence), *Bōei kenshūjo senshishitsu* (Defence Research War History Section), *Senshi sōsho, dai honei rikugun bu* (War History Series, Central Headquarters, Army Section (1)), Asagumo Shinbunsha, 1967.
8 Ibid., pp. 453–4.

Chapter 10

1. *Ogawa Heikichi kankei bunsho* (Documents concerning Ogawa Heikichi), vol. 2, pp. 146–7.
2. *Hara Kei nikki* (Hara Kei Diary), p. 145.
3. Ibid., p. 146.
4. Ibid., pp. 140–1.
5. Ibid., p. 141.
6. *Hara Kei nikki* (Hara Kei Diary), vol. 5, p. 276.
7. Ibid., p. 297.
8. The overriding power of the Emperor and foreign policy power.
9. The Emperor had the Supreme Command of the army and navy.
10. *Suzuki Sadakazu danwa sokkiroku* (Stenographic record of conversation with Suzuki Sadakazu), final volume, pp. 378–9. No more information on the Web.
11. *Taiheiyō sensō e no michi* (The Road to the Pacific War), separate volume of materials, pp. 159–60.
12. *Saionji kō to seikyoku* (Prince Saionji and the Political Situation), vol. 2, p. 141.
13. *Gendai shi shiryō, zoku: Manshū jihen* (Materials in Modern History, Continuation: The Manchurian Incident), p. 280.
14. *Nihon gaikō bunsho: Manshū jihen* (Japanese Foreign Policy Documents: Manchurian Incident), vol. 1, Chapter 3, p. 118.
15. *Taiheiyō sensō e no michi, bekkan shiryō hen* (The Road to the Pacific War, Separate Materials Volume), p. 162.
16. The monthly journal *Kaizō*, September 1937.

Conclusion

1. Ibid. Nagai Kazu, *Nitchū sensō kara sekai sensō e* (*From the Japan-China War to World War*) (Kyōto: Shibunkaku Shuppan, 2007), p. 349.
2. Ibid., pp. 298–9.
3. *Ogawa Heikichi kankei bunsho* (Documents concerning Ogawa Heikichi), vol. 1, p. 652.
4. Ibid., vol. 2, p. 435.
5. Ibid., p. 343.
6. Ibid., p. 344.
7. Ibid., p. 344.
8. Ibid., p. 357.
9. Ibid., p. 358.
10. Ibid.
11. Ibid., p. 356.

Index

Page numbers with "n" refer to endnotes.

2-26 Incident 146
  influence of 124–6
5-15 Incident 118, 122–4, 126, 146
'1923 crisis' 69–70, 72

Abe government 159
Abolition of the General Staff Office
  133–7
abortive Ugaki Kazushige Cabinet
  126, 149
administrative retrenchment 94
Aikokusha (Patriotic Society) 18
Akashi Motojirō 107–9, 119
alienation 23–4
America 66, 67, 70, 72, 85, 88, 92, 108,
  109, 119, 120
  disdain for 107–9
Americanization 43, 45
Anglo-Japanese Alliance 61–2, 117
anti-Japanese sentiment 154–5
anti-Japan faction in Korea 29
Araki Sadao 118
Arisugawa no Miya Taruhito 34
armed conflict, with China 86
army expenditures 39
army faction 86, 91
Army High Command 145
Army Ministry 145
army rearmament 60, 72, 73, 76, 77
  funding of 74
Asianism of Fukuzawa Yukichi 27–9, 32
authoritarian thought 146

Banno, Junji
  Meiji demokurashii (*Meiji
    Democracy*) 21
  Meiji kenpō taisei no kakuritsu (*The
    Establishment of the Meiji
    Constitutional System*) 58
  Nihon kindai shi (*Modern Japanese
    History*) 38

Shôwa shi no ketteiteki shunkan
  (*Decisive Moments in Shôwa
  History*) 38
Boshin War 9, 11
Boxer Rebellion 63, 65
British political system 23
broad-based defence 146–7
budget 38–40, 73, 76, 91, 94, 96–100, 109
bunmei kaika 15
business tax 80–1

cabinet decisions 127–9
censure motion 96, 98
Chambers of Commerce 80, 87, 93, 94
Chemulp'o Treaty 30
Chiang Kai Shek 154–7
China 67, 70, 72, 92, 107, 122
  disdain for 107–9
  policy 136
    fundamental shift in 132–3
  special rights in 108
  strong power 29–30, 32
  threat argument 25–6
  three divisions to 129–30
  underestimation of 27–9, 41
Chinese civilization 31
Chinese Communist Party 155
  growing strength 156–7
Chinese military system 33
Chinese modernization 28, 29
Chinese Revolution in 1911 87
Chōshū faction 34–5
Chūō Kurabu 89
Chūseikai 54, 93, 98, 99, 101, 105, 110
'circumstances of relations between
  the military and the Foreign
  Ministry concerning the
  Manchurian issue, The' 139
'collapse of the Yamamoto Cabinet and
  the establishment of the Ōkuma
  Cabinet, The' (Yoshino) 102

collective defence 159
communist guerrillas 156, 157
'Conditions in Occupied Territory, The' (Ogawa) 155
conflicts of interest, pluralization of 81
conservatism 19–20, 55. *See also* radicalism
conservative faction 24, 38, 39
Constitution 1–5
    clash between Empire and 138–9
    continuation of 37
    key points of 104
    and non-Empire 131–2
    towards an Empire 105–6
Constitutional Democrats 159
constitutionalism 1–4, 131–2
Constitutionalists 159
'Constitution at home, Empire abroad' 2, 53
Constitution Defence Movement 83, 90, 109
'Constitution domestically' concept 54–5, 72, 73, 101
'Constitution in domestic policy' 54–5
constitution period 16–17
corporation tax, reduction in 93, 94

Daidō danketsu movement 105
Dalian (Dairen) 64–8, 107
Debuchi Katsuji 143, 144
defence policy 76, 120
Defence Research Bureau Office on the History of War 75
democracy 1, 5, 82–3, 102, 110, 117, 147, 149
    Great War and 117
    peace and (*see* peace and democracy)
    to stop war 147–8
    Taishō 53–4, 72–4, 83, 115
democratization movement, progress of 82–3
Den Kenjirō 98, 99
Diet, military expansion 37–9
'Diplomatic Misunderstandings and the Extension of the Manchurian Incident' 139
domain-faction government 21
Dōshikai 98, 99, 110
'Down with the Domain-Clique, defend Constitutionalism' 82, 89

'Edict to Establish a Constitutional Regime' 1
eight-year rearmament plan 60
electoral law 82, 101–2
    revision of 79–80
emergence of urban commerce and industry 79–81
Emperor
    absolutism 37–8
    constitutionalism 37
    power 74
Emperor for the Military Command 74–5
Empire 1–5, 14
    birth of 37
    clash between Constitution and 138–9
    Constitution did not aspire to 57–8
    from Constitution to 105–6
    counterattack in favour of 136–7
'Empire externally' concept 54–6, 73, 101, 110, 118
'Empire in foreign policy' 54–5, 58
epochs, extinction of 145–6
establishment of a Parliament, postponing 23–4
Europeanization 42–5
extinction of epochs 145–6

fascism 146, 147
financial policy 30, 73, 81, 94
financial retrenchment 38–40
First Constitutional Defence Movement. *See* Taishō Political Crisis
First World War 63, 69–70, 82, 108–11, 116–18, 131, 135
    German defeat in 134
    twenty-one demands to China 106–7
Forbes 141, 144
foreign minister 125–8
Foreign Ministry 145
foreign policy 37, 39, 46, 65, 110, 123–5, 134, 136, 141, 145
    power 110, 126, 145, 148, 149
    prerogative 148
France 50, 66, 67, 70, 119
fukoku kyōhei 15, 25, 26, 28, 41
Fukuzawa Yukichi 16, 18–21, 23–4, 30–3
    Asianism of 27–9, 32
    Heiron 31, 32, 34
    Inoue Kaoru and 21–3
    Jiji Shinpō 28, 33, 34

Jiji shōgen 27, 28, 31
  reforming Korea 32–3
Fukuzawa Yukichi zenshū 21–2, 34
full-scale war without a war declaration 129–30
Furusawa Shigeru 14–15
future enemies 66. *See also* potential enemies

general elections of March 1915 109–10
General Staff Office 4, 137
  Abolition of the 133–7
Germany 66, 67, 70, 108
Great Britain 43, 45, 49, 108, 119
Great Depression 122–3
Great Japan Imperial Constitution. *See* Meiji Constitution

Hamada Kunimatsu 146
Hamaguchi Osachi 5, 117, 120, 121, 123, 124, 126, 132, 136, 139
Hanabusa Yoshimoto 26–7
Harada Kumao 140
Hara Kei 56, 58, 59, 62, 89, 90, 93, 94, 96, 100, 109–10, 117, 118, 133–6, 139, 148
  Constitution and non-Empire under 131–2
Heiron (On the Military, Fukuzawa) 31, 32, 34
Hermann 95–6
Hibiya Arson Incident 83
Hidaka 128
Hirota Kōki 128
House of Councillors 55, 99, 100
House of Peers 78, 79, 99, 100
  power of 97
  revenge of the 97–9
House of Representatives 42–5, 57, 73, 76, 78, 79, 82, 93, 98, 100, 148
  1914 budget 96, 99–100
  censure motion 96, 98
  decision of 97
  and the government, dispute in 39–41
  land tax and 60–2
  power of 97
  rearmament plans for army and navy 60
Hŭngsŏn Taewŏngun 29

Iaku jōsō 74–6
'If war breaks out, victory is assured' 33–4
Ii Naosuke 123
Ijichi Masaharu 11
Imo (Jingo) Incident 29–32, 45
Imperial Constitution. *See* Meiji Constitution
Imperial Defence Plan 95
Imperial Defence Policy 66–7, 69–72, 74, 76, 77, 84, 88, 91–2, 107, 120, 122, 158
Iaku jōsō 74–6
Imperial Edict 3
  Constitutional Regime 101
  ending of the constitutional period 16–17
  to establish a Constitutional Regime 16, 20, 24
  on Harmony and Cooperation 41–2, 45
Imperial House 134
imperialism 1–3, 82, 88, 110, 136, 137, 145
imperialist diplomacy 69
Imperial Order 121, 124, 142
Imperial Rescript of 1875 5
Independence of Korea 65, 68
independent access to the Emperor 134, 135, 137, 139
Inoue Kaoru 14–15, 18, 23–4, 34, 35, 89
  Fukuzawa Yukichi and 21–3
  miscalculation by 18–21
Inoue Kiyoshi 40
Inoue Kowashi 20, 21, 125
Integrity of China 65, 68
Integrity of Korea 65, 68
interest groups 82, 87
Inukai Tsuyoshi 45, 47, 93, 101, 105, 118, 119, 123, 145
Ise Shrine 47–8
Ishiwara Kanji 122, 138
Itagaki Taisuke 10, 11, 14–16, 18, 21
  popular assembly argument 19
Itō Hirobumi 15, 20–3, 40, 41, 43, 45–8, 58, 62, 74, 75, 125, 157
  avoidance of war by 34–6
Itō Takashi 160
Iwakura Mission 15
Iwakura Tomomi 20, 34

Japan
  from the army to the navy 90–2
  constitutional government 1
  democratization movement, progress of 82–3
  expansion plan for the army and navy 71–2
  financial policy 81
  nationalization of tax system 80–1
  potential enemies of 66–8, 70–2
  three army divisions 126–9
  war with America 2, 158
Japan–China confrontation 14, 26–7, 32, 129
  over Ryūkyū 11–12
Japan–China peace settlement 153–4
Japan–China Treaty 49–50
Japan–China War 9–11, 72, 127, 149, 153, 155, 157, 158–60
  democracy to stop 147–8
  lengthy war of attrition 150–1
  as national liberation war 150
Japanese Army 119, 149, 151
  divisions 71, 84–8, 105
  warships 71
Japanese economy 81
  growth 133
Japanese Navy 33, 48, 61, 66, 95
Japanese politics 87, 102, 110, 111
Japan–Korea relations 26–7
Japan–Russia Agreement 72
Japan–Russia Peace Treaty 64, 68
Japan Sea Naval War 70
Japan's Korean Army 70
Japan–Soviet relations 152
Japan–US Alliance 158
Japan–US Mutual Security Treaty 159
Jiji Shinpō (Fukuzawa) 28, 33, 34
Jiji shōgen (Fukuzawa) 27, 28, 31
Jin Province 139–45
Jiyūtō 38, 40–4, 57, 58, 60, 76, 79, 92

Kadota Jun 66, 75
Kaishintō 38, 40, 41, 43, 47, 57, 105
Kakushin Club 55
Kanaya Hanzō 121, 122, 139–41, 143, 145
  non-expansion policy 142
Kaneko Kentarō 79
Kanghwado Incident 17–18
Kanghwado Treaty of 1876 18, 26

Kantōgun 61, 118, 120–2, 127, 133, 137–9, 141–5, 148
  control of 139–41
Kapsin (Kōshin) Incident 32–3, 35, 45
Katō Hiroharu 120
Katō Takaaki 55, 101, 103, 110, 117
Katsura Cabinet 59, 61–2, 73, 85–6, 88–92
  no-confidence motion against 90, 96
Katsura New Party 88, 92, 94, 105
Katsura–Saionji system 78–9
Katsura Tarō 59, 61, 62, 73, 78–9, 85–6, 88–92, 96–8, 105
Kawamura Sumiyoshi 12, 30, 34
Kenseihontō 62
Kenseikai 54, 88, 103, 110, 117, 118, 136
Kenseitō 58, 62, 79
  diplomacy failure 117–19
Kido Kōin 10, 11, 14–16, 19, 24, 152, 157
Koizumi Nobukichi 19
Koizumi Shinkichi 28
Kōjunsha 20–1, 23
Kokkai kisei dōmei 18
Kokumin Kyōkai 42–3
Kokumin Shinbun 86
Kokumintō 88–90, 93, 98, 99, 105
Kōmei (Emperor of Japan) 47–8
Komura Jūtarō 64
Komuro Shinobu 14–15
Kondō Shinsuke 29
Konoe Atsumaro 152, 153
Konoe Fumimaro 127–9, 152–4
Korea 61
  anti-Japan faction in 29
  assimilation of 84
  becoming a protectorate 64–6, 70
  breakdown in the reform of 32–3
  Japanese legation 35
  pro-China faction in 27, 32
  pro-Japan faction in 27, 29, 32, 33
  protection 35
Kōtoku Shūsui 62
Kōyū Club 54
Kuomintang Government 154
Kuroda Kiyotaka 9–12
Kwantung Army 70
Kwantung lease agreement 68

land tax 57, 58, 60–2
Lee Hung Chang 36, 48, 49
Liaodong Peninsula 48–50, 57, 61

Liberation of Korea 65
Liutiaokou Incident of 18 September 1931 119
London Naval Disarmament Treaty 5, 118, 120–1, 123, 126, 138
Lushun (Ryōjun) 64–8, 107
Lytton Commission report 155

Manchukuo, formal recognition of 119
Manchuria 53, 56, 61, 63, 120
   development of 85
   military authorities in 143
   nine-article treaty on 106
   partition of 64–6
   plan to take over 137–8
   political control over 122
   privileges to 69–70, 72, 79
   Russian occupation 65
   special rights to 68–70, 72, 79, 86, 105–8, 116, 117, 136
Manchurian (Liutiaokou) Incident 2, 5, 117–19, 121–3, 126, 138, 140, 141, 145, 146, 152, 153, 155–6
   clash between Constitution and Empire 138–9
   preventing an expansion of 144
Marco Polo Bridge Incident 2, 119, 126–9
Masaki Jinzaburō 124
mass demonstration movements 83, 92, 97
mass movement 151
mass street movements 91
Masuda Kenji 160
Matsukata Masayoshi 30, 34
Matsumoto Seichō, *Ten to sen* (Points and Lines) 149
Matsumoto Yawara 95–6
Matsuo Takayoshi 53–4, 73
media 97–9
Meiji Constitution 4, 40, 58, 97, 100, 129
   Article 9 158
   Article 11 4, 74, 75, 120, 127, 137, 144, 148
   Article 12 74–6, 120
   Article 13 110, 125, 137, 145, 148, 149
   article 55 161 n.3
   Article 64 97
   Article 65 97
Meiji constitutionalism 24

Meiji demokurashii (*Meiji Democracy*, Banno) 21
Meiji Emperor 1, 16
   opposition to Sino-Japanese War 46–8
Meiji government 12, 16, 24, 27
   split in 9–11
Meiji kenpō taisei no kakuritsu (*The Establishment of the Meiji Constitutional System*, Banno) 58
Meiji Restoration of 1868 1, 11, 12, 16, 21, 65, 104, 123, 138
Meiji tennō ki (*Life of the Meiji Emperor*) 47
middle-ranking officers 137–8
militarism 135
military
   achievements 149, 150
   disarmament treaty 120
   rearmament 86–8
military expansion
   before launching the Diet 37–9
   stagnation of 39–41
Minami Jirō 121, 122, 139–41, 145
ministers of state 127
   responsibility 161 n.3
Minjō isshin 20
Minobe Tatsukichi 4, 75, 134
Minponshugi (Yoshino) 53–4
minryoku kyūyō 76
Minseitō Cabinet 55, 88, 118–27, 129, 132, 136, 138, 139, 141, 146
Mitsui Bussan 96
Mongolia 53, 56, 64, 120
   development of 85
   nine-article treaty on 106
   plan to take over 137–8
   political control over 122
   special rights to 69–70, 72, 79, 86, 107, 108, 116, 117, 136
Mutsu Munemitsu 43, 45–8

Nagai Kazu, *Nitchû sensô kara sekai sensô e* (*From Japan-China War to World War*) 150–1
Nagata Tetsuzan 138
Naigai kokusaku shiken (*A Personal Opinion on Domestic and Foreign Policy*, Takahashi) 133–4
Nakamigawa Hikojirō 19, 22

Nakano Buei 80, 93
Nakazato Hiroshi 61–2
Nakazato Yūji 73
Nanjing 128, 149, 152–4, 157
narrow defence 147
national defence 86, 148
nationalism 41, 42–5
nationalization of tax system 80–1
Naval Command Office 4
Naval Disarmament Treaty 135–6
naval rearmament 30–2, 41, 58, 60, 73, 76, 77, 85–7, 92, 94, 95, 97, 120
  and expansion 94
  funding of 74
  funds for 91
  speed up of 61–2
  spending for 100
  ten-year plan for 60–2
naval stratagems 70–1
navy cabinet, collapse of 99–100
navy expenditures 39
navy faction 91
new Empire faction 118, 120
new Meiji government, split in 9–11
new world order 116
Nicholas II 64
Nihon kindai shi (*Modern Japanese History*, Banno) 38
Nitchû sensô kara sekai sensô e (*From Japan-China War to World War*, Nagai) 150–1
no-compensation peace treaty 73
Noda Utarō 89
Nonaka Shirō 125
non-expansion policy, breakdown of 144–5
'non-imperial' policies 137
non-*Seiyūkai* Cabinet 101
non-*Seiyūkai* Party 110

Ogawa Heikichi 10, 151–3, 155–7, 160
  'Conditions in Occupied Territory, The' 155
  peace settlement opinion 153–4
  Waga kanmi (Personal opinion) 152
Ogawa Heikichi kankei bunsho 160
Okada Keisuke 124
Ōkubo Toshimichi 10, 14, 16–18, 26, 35, 152, 153, 157
Ōkuma Shigenobu 16, 17, 21, 22, 38, 101, 102, 104–6, 109, 110

old Empire faction 118, 120
Ōsaka Conference 14–16, 18
overriding foreign policy power 145, 149
Ōyama Iwao 34
Ozaki Yukio 93, 101, 105

Park Yŏnghyo 32
partition of Manchuria 64–6
party cabinets 5, 55, 73, 82, 103, 121, 126, 139, 140, 146, 148, 149
  death of 122–4
peace and democracy 118, 131
  split between 109–11
  system of apportionment 53–6
peace movement 159
peace negotiations 48
peace settlement 150–1, 155, 157
  opinion 153–4
Peking Government 68
Peking Treaty 66
People's Government 154, 155, 157
Perry, Matthew C. 9, 28
pluralization of conflicts of interest 81
policy failure 121–2
political progress 82
popularism 38
popular movement 96, 98, 99
Popular Rights Movement 17–18, 57, 82
Portsmouth Treaty. *See* Japan–Russia Peace Treaty
positive policies
  and rearmament 76–8
  Yamamoto Gonbei 92–4
post-Sino-Japanese War Management 60
potential enemies 66–8, 70–2, 85, 92, 107, 108, 120, 122
pre-war Japan 3–5, 20, 37, 55, 127, 139, 159
prime minister 122, 124, 126–9
  power of 139
  responsibility 161 n.3
private railways 77
Privilege of the High Command 122, 127
Privy Council (*Sūmitsuin*) 91, 120
pro-China faction in Korea 27, 32
pro-Japan faction in Korea 27, 29, 32, 33
'prosperous country, strong army' (*fukoku kyōhei*) 15, 25, 26, 28, 41, 43, 58, 61
Provisional Government 154

public opinion 35, 44, 88–90, 97, 109, 144–6, 149
  navy and army 85–6
Pu Yi 138, 155

quasi-party cabinets 149

radical faction 21, 38, 39
  movement 18
radicalism 20
railways
  extension 76–7
  nationalization 77–8
rapprochement of the army 105
real potential enemies 67–8
rearmament 60–2, 71–3
  army (see army rearmament)
  naval (see naval rearmament)
  positive policy and 76–8
reforming Korea 32–3
Regular Chinese Forces 145
Rengō article 143
representative system 38
Restoration Government 154
right to vote 82
Rikken Dōshikai 54, 88, 93, 101, 105
Rikken Kokumintō 93, 101
Rinpō heibi ryaku (Military Preparations and Strategy of Neighbouring Powers, Yamagata) 32
Russia 49–50, 92, 107, 108, 119
  Japan went to war with 63–4
Russo-Japanese War 2, 55, 57–61, 63–4, 70–4, 77, 79, 85–7, 92, 107, 138, 158
  Constitution after the 90
  electoral law in 82
  financial difficulties after 77
  Hibiya Arson Incident at 83
  Japanese victory in 63–5, 68, 69
  Katsura–Saionji system 78–9
  'no war' argument in 62
  partition of Manchuria and 64–6
  peace treaty after 72
  result of 67–8, 70
  special tax during 80, 84
  tax threshold in 82
Ryūkyū, Japan–China War over 11–12

Saigō Takamori 10–12, 17
Saigō Tsugumichi 12, 34
Saionji Kinmochi 73, 75–9, 85–8, 90–1, 93–4, 98, 100, 105, 124, 140
Saionji-Katsura regime 55
Saitō Makoto 124
Saitō Takao 125, 146
Sanjō Sanetomi 9, 34
Sat-Chō (Satsuma-Chōshū)
  government 34
Second World War 115, 116, 135.
  See also First World War
secret agreement 61–3, 72
security policy 159
Seiyūkai 54–5, 57–8, 62, 73, 76–81, 85, 86, 88–90, 92–4, 96, 98, 101–5, 109, 110, 117–20, 123, 124, 126, 127, 129, 131, 136, 139, 145–6, 148
  collapse of navy cabinet and 99–100
  extreme violence of 105
  great conversion of 117
sekkyokushugi 76
self-defence 148
Self-Defence Forces 159
Senkaku islands 158, 159
Senryōchijijō (the situation in the Occupied Areas) 156
Shakai Taishūtō (Social Masses Party), upsurge of 146–7
Shandong Province 106
  German rights to 108, 116, 131
Shidehara Kijūrō 122, 139–45
  diplomacy 55, 121
  failure of 117–19
Shimonoseki Treaty. See Japan-China Peace Treaty
Shinpotō 58, 62
Shogunate 10
Shōwa history 75, 115, 138
Shôwa shi no ketteiteki shunkan (Decisive Moments in Shôwa History, Banno) 38
Siemens corruption affair 73, 83, 92, 94–7
Sino-Japanese Peace Treaty 66
Sino-Japanese War 2, 44–6, 55–9, 62, 65, 70, 73, 74, 85–6, 92, 152, 155.
  See also Russo-Japanese War
  conclusion of 48–9
  demands 48–9

expansion of army and navy 60–1
opposition from the Meiji Emperor 46–8
Sorai Mamoru 160
special contingency tax 84
'split over subduing Korea' 10
Stimson, Henry 121, 139, 141, 142, 144
  failure 142–4
strange political party 109–11
strong army argument 25–6
strong power, China 29–30, 32
'subdue Korea' argument 10, 12
Sugita Teiichi 77
Sugiyama Hajime 128
supreme power 74–5
Suzuki Teiichi 137
system of apportionment, peace and democracy 53–6

Taiseitō-Seiyūkai 54
Taishō Democracy 53–4, 83, 115
  resistance and compromise 72–4
Taishō Political Change 71, 78
Taishō Political Crisis 88–91, 101
Taishō seikyoku shi ron (Sohō) 97
Taiwan expedition
  of 1874 1, 2, 5, 9–11, 13, 14, 16, 25, 26, 34, 37, 92, 132, 148, 153, 158, 160
    Japan–China War over Ryūkyū 11–12
  of 1894 157
Takahashi Korekiyo 56, 94, 124, 131–3, 139, 148
  Abolition of the General Staff Office 133–7
  Naigai kokusaku shiken (A Personal Opinion on Domestic and Foreign Policy) 133–4
  statement of opinion 134, 135
Takarabe Takeshi 95–6
Takezoe Shinichirō 32
Tanaka Giichi 55, 66, 70, 85, 87, 88, 105, 107, 117, 135–7
  counterattack in favour of Empire 136–7
taxation 62, 68, 77, 84
tax system, nationalization of 80–1
tax threshold 82

Ten to sen (Points and Lines, Matsumoto) 149
ten-year rearmament plan 60–2
Terauchi Hisaichi 146
Terauchi Masatake 87, 105, 108
three anti-Seiyūkai factions 101–5
Thursday Society (Mokuyōkai) 137, 138
Tianjin Treaty 34–6, 38, 39, 44–5
Tientsingun 148
Tōa Dōbunkai (East Asia Same Script Society) 152
Tōgō Heihachirō 64
Tōjō Hideki 122, 138
Tokudaiji Sanetsune 46
  Taishō seikyoku shi ron 97
Tonghak Party 44, 45
Tosaka Jun 147, 148
Tōyama Mitsuru 10, 152–3, 157
  peace negotiations 12–13
Treaty of Friendship. See Kanghwado Treaty of 1876
Triple Intervention 49–50, 57
'Twenty-one Demands' 2, 106–10, 116, 117
  demanding withdrawal of 119
twin deficits 84–5
'tyranny of party men' 87

Uehara Yūsaku 71, 86, 88
Ueki Emori 20
Ugaki Kazushige 126–9, 140, 146, 149
unfortunate chain of small mistakes 141–2
Universal Male Suffrage Law of 1925 3, 55, 72, 82, 104
universal suffrage 3, 5, 54, 103, 104, 110–11, 117, 120, 131, 148
  bill against 132
  electors 148
  Yoshino Sakuzō 102–5
urban commerce and industry 79–81
US Secretary of State 143

Wade 13
Waga kanmi (Personal opinion, Ogawa) 152
Wakatsuki Reijirō 5, 117–19, 121, 124, 132, 139, 145
Wang 128
war achievements 150

wartime nationalism   151
Washington Conference in 1921 and
    1922   116
Washington Treaty (February 1922)   110
Watanabe Jōtarō   124
Western Great Powers   152
White Vote Association   90
Wilson, Woodrow   108
Witte, Sergei   64

Yamada Akiyoshi   34
Yamagata Aritomo   10, 11, 15, 25–7, 29,
    32–4, 66–8, 70, 72, 85, 97, 105,
    109, 119, 122, 134, 135, 153,
    157, 158
    '1923 crisis'   69–70, 72
    revision of the election law   79–80

Rinpō heibi ryaku   32
Yamamoto Gonbei   91, 92, 99, 100, 105
    positive policies   92–4
    Siemens Affair and   94–7
Yellow Sea Naval War   70
Yonai Mitsumasa   128
Yosano Akiko   62
Yoshino Sakuzō   4–5, 55, 73, 83, 105–7
    'collapse of the Yamamoto Cabinet and
        the establishment of the Ōkuma
        Cabinet, The'   102
    Minponshugi   53–4
    non-*Seiyūkai* parties   109
    rise of   101–2
    three non-*Seiyūkai* factions   101–5
    universal suffrage   5, 102–5
Yuan Shih-Kai   30, 32, 106–7

www.ingramcontent.com/pod-product-compliance
Lightning Source LLC
Chambersburg PA
CBHW061836300426
44115CB00013B/2412